Leading Collaborative Organizations

Leading Collaborative Organizations

Insights into Guiding Horizontal Organizations

By

Tyrus Ross Clayton

Emeritus Professor of the USC Price School of Public Policy
Formerly Dean of the USC School of Public Administration

With An Appendix On Public Private Partnerships
By

John Shirey

City Manager, Sacramento

iUniverse LLC
Bloomington

Leading Collaborative Organizations
Insights into Guiding Horizontal Organizations

iUniverse books may be ordered through booksellers or by contacting:

iUniverse LLC
1663 Liberty Drive
Bloomington, IN 47403
www.iuniverse.com
1-800-Authors (1-800-288-4677)

ISBN: 978-1-4917-1022-7 (sc)
ISBN: 978-1-4917-1024-1 (hc)
ISBN: 978-1-4917-1023-4 (e)

Library of Congress Control Number: 2013918774

Printed in the United States of America.

iUniverse rev. date: 10/26/2013

CONTENTS

LIST OF FIGURES

To

Individuals who have worked, now work, or will work in the
public, private, and not-for-profit sectors and have dedicated
or will dedicate part of their lives to public service.

Preface and Acknowledgements

Readers may better understand this writer's perspectives as expressed in this book if they understand my previous experiences which led to the decision to write a book on the topic of providing leadership in collaborative organizations.

In my two years of graduate study at the University of California at Los Angeles I took courses in the Political Science Department while pursuing the Master of Public Administration degree. During those years I worked in the Bureau of Government Research on a metropolitan governance research project. A particular focus of that project was the Lakewood Contract Plan. Lakewood was a post-World War II phenomenon. Thousands of new homes had been constructed in an unincorporated area just to the north of the City of Long Beach. Residents of Lakewood voted to incorporate, but did not have a very substantial tax base. A decision was made to contract with the County of Los Angeles for public safety services. Lakewood became the first "Contract City"; many other newly incorporated cities followed their lead. This collaborative effort between governments became an important focus for academic research and a long term interest of mine.

My first significant exposure to organizational theory and analysis occurred in this context. I learned to appreciate that there are multiple ways to organize and attain predictable patterns of behavior. I also learned that market models of organized activity were at least as powerful as the more established bureaucratic models, and systems models were emerging that promised to bring novel insights to leaders of organizations. I developed an appreciation for the power of the conceptual tools and languages being employed by different academic disciplines. My interest in organizational arrangements has been continuous since those experiences at UCLA.

I spent the first eight years after receiving my MPA working as a Management Analyst at a Research and Development Laboratory at China Lake, California. My home base while there was the Central Staff Department; this vantage point provided me an opportunity to gain an understanding of the Laboratory as a whole and the nature of the Research, Development, Test, and Evaluation cycle.

My office loaned me on two occasions to assist with the management of project teams. I was able to observe first-hand how ideas are generated, inventions are brought into being, and innovation of those inventions takes place. I also became familiar with the problems and issues that confront project leaders who are expected to lead the work of their teams even though many of their key project personnel are not direct reports. In fact, many of them were not even employees of the laboratory; they worked for other organizations around the country. I came to understand that it takes exceptional leadership abilities to guide project teams in the absence of hierarchical based authority.

During these eight years, I took an educational fellowship from the laboratory and spent 15 months as a full time student at the University of Southern California's School of Public Administration. By the end of fifteen months I had passed all preliminary and qualifying examinations and was advanced to candidacy for the Ph. D, in Public Administration. I returned to China Lake for another 3 years. At that point I was invited by then Director, Frank Sherwood, to join the faculty of the School of Public Administration for a two year appointment. During those two years I wrote my dissertation which addressed the thorny issues involved in evaluation of R&D Laboratories.

At the time my two year contract with USC was ending, the School's Director, David Mars, made me an offer to become a long term member of the faculty. I spent the rest of my academic career at

USC, and still consider the Price School of Public Policy to be my professional home.

The School of Public Administration was a Professional School with an interdisciplinary faculty. While it had faculty with interests in politics and public policy, I found it most attuned to organizational and managerial research. There were many in-service students along with younger pre-service students. The Professors were directly engaged with working professionals and quite involved with their problems and issues. The faculty also had a deep commitment to their students and took great pride in having created a "learning community"; excellent teaching was as prized as quality research, and public service was a given. Assisting in the development of Public Leaders was a central part of the School's mission.

It was not at all surprising that the Federal Government would turn to USC Professors Frank Sherwood and Chester Newland to develop and guide their Federal Executive Institute (FEI). Over the years many other USC faculty and alumni have served on the staff of the FEI. I spent a very enjoyable year on the FEI faculty, teaching courses on science and public policy, organizational aging, and group problem solving.

My continuing teaching interests during the years I was not serving as an academic administrator included organizational theory and analysis, administrative systems analysis, and research and development administration (including science and public policy). The years I spent serving as Dean of the School of Public Administration-1982-1991, and the years I spent as Director of the University's campus in Sacramento also have impacted the content of this book.

While Dean, I found it necessary to make some pivotal changes in the School's operation. To bring more stability to enrollments, I encouraged the broadening of the School's curriculum in the areas of health administration and public policy. Financial and University realities led me to focus considerable energy on building an endowment for the School. To do this I established a Development

Office and helped a talented staff member, Christine Glogow, grow into one of the University's finest Development Officers. Together, we formed the School's Board of Councilors to aid us with making the School more visible and better able to raise funds.

Working with the Board, which included a number of private sector CEO's, gave me a better appreciation of the extent to which private sector organizations take their public responsibilities quite seriously. These Board members were extremely helpful to the School each year in the planning and delivery of our major fundraising dinner, the "Ides of March".

A not-for-profit CEO, Leonard Schaeffer, agreed to my request to come on the School's Board and asked that in exchange, I join his Blue Cross of California Consumer Relations and Public Policy committees. I enjoyed my service with this not-for-profit corporation and stayed with it until a few years after I had stepped down as Dean. Even though I worked for a not-for-profit corporation, USC, the experience with Blue Cross and the Foundations it formed after converting to a for-profit status was enlightening in terms my having been directly engaged in a collaborative health organization.

After spending some years as a retiree, I was asked if I would be willing to teach a graduate course on Inter-sectoral Leadership. My understanding was the course was in need of "retooling", and that I would have the opportunity to come up with my own approach to the subject matter. I accepted the challenge. I first taught the course as an "intensive" which meant teaching this 2 unit course over two week-ends; it involved 32 classroom hours. Subsequently, I taught the course in an on-line format over a period of 15 weeks. Paul Danczyk joined me as a co-teacher; we each had two sections as there were a total of 65 students enrolled in the course.

While designing the curriculum and selecting the readings for the Inter-sectoral Leadership class, it became apparent that there was a need for a book that specifically addressed the subject of the class. I decided that I would take on the challenge to produce a short book intended to assist individuals already participating in inter-sectoral collaborative organizations and pre-service students preparing themselves for their possible participation in collaborative organizations.

I have identified the premises underlying the book in Chapter 1, so I will not include them here. I will note that the book is rooted in literature on leadership, and on organizational theory and analysis. I want to acknowledge that I chose not to make the book scholarly in the sense of documenting sources used in great bibliographic detail. I do provide information on authors, book titles and Journal articles that make it possible for readers to readily "Google" these sources when more detail is desired, and hope that they will be stimulated to read some of the publications discussed in this book.

My late wife, Luanne Clayton, was very much involved with my class preparations and delivery; she was an insightful critic and a source of constant encouragement. I loved her greatly and thank her for the fifty-six years we spent together. Our daughter, Carolyn, once again has used her computer literacy and substantial experience in management consulting to polish this manuscript and ready it for publishing. Both have my gratitude and love.

I wish to acknowledge the Director, faculty and staff of the USC Center in Sacramento for their assistance as I taught the two courses noted above. Chester Newland was particularly supportive, and Paul Danczyk an exceptionally able co-teacher for the on-line class.

John Shirey, City Manager of Sacramento, visited both of these classes and presented his insights into principles to bear in mind when entering into public-private partnerships. John graciously accepted my invitation to prepare the appendix to this book that addresses public private partnerships; these partnerships have become one of the more important forms of collaborative organization. I am grateful to John for sharing his experience-based insights into this organizational form.

Perhaps, most of all, I am indebted to the USC graduate students who sat through the two courses and provided feedback on the materials covered in the class. I particularly enjoyed one of their evaluative comments. Let me paraphrase it: I worked so hard for this course; it should have carried 4 units of credit, but I like that fact that I only had to pay for 2 units of tuition and received 4 units of education!

TRC
Rocklin, California
2013

Chapter 1

Overview

Background

When private sector organizations or local, state and national governments are experiencing problems, the blame is often attributed to failed leadership. In such circumstances, leaders receive most of the criticism even though economic, political and other factors may be as much as, or more responsible for these problems. The truth is that mono-causal explanations of often difficult, interdependent problems oversimplify complex realities. Nonetheless, effective leadership is very important to both avoidance of problems and the solution of those problems when they occur.

This importance is magnified in "Collaborative Organizations". Providing leadership in a collaborative organization is somewhat like trying to influence the behaviors of all individuals on a raft in white water given the noise, turbulent flow of the water and the different vantage points, assets and concerns of the crewmembers.

Leadership is particularly important when two or more organizations from different sectors (Private, Public and Not-for Profit) agree to collaboratively undertake programs or projects that cannot be carried out by a single sector. As these collaborative efforts are formed, partnerships between organizations lead to collaborative organizational activity and in essence, new "organizations" with notable characteristics are brought into being in often loosely structured arrangements. Mechanisms such as contracts, mutual aid agreements, terms of agreement, memoranda of understanding, public-private partnerships etc. are put into place. These arrangements create many leadership challenges. The primary purpose of this book is to aid leaders working in collaborative organizations to meet these challenges.

I had an opportunity to personally experience the dynamics of a collaborative organization early in my career. I was asked to become a temporary member of a project team that was in the formative stage of its project life cycle. The project had as it charge, development of a missile to exploit a novel guidance concept that had been benched tested. This project team included individuals who worked at various government laboratories scattered around the country and some consultants from the private sector. Only a few of the team's members were direct reports of the Engineer selected to be the project's manager. This Engineer was tasked to coordinate this ever-growing team's efforts; however he was not empowered with those elements of authority commonly associated with individuals occupying positions within a hierarchy.

My assignment on this team was to help develop a time and cost plan for the project using the then novel PERT planning technology (Program Evaluation and Review Technique). In the process of gathering information for this plan I visited the various engineering groups that were working separately on their tasks related to the different missile elements: the guidance and control systems, the airframe and its skin, the missile's power source, its explosive component, the missile's aerodynamic characteristics, studies of its manufacturability and reliability, and missile testing and evaluation procedures.

The centrality of the Project Manager's role quickly became apparent. These differing groups of Engineers were starting their work employing different assumptions about the eventual missile's length, weight, and center of gravity as well as their time and cost assumptions. I was able to provide clear evidence of the important role of the project manager as the missile's master architect and facilitator of team communications to ensure all were on the same page. Team members readily grasped the importance of working from common assumptions and recognized their mutual interdependence as their work progressed. The project team understood that collaboration was crucial and that the Project manager's role was central. In the ensuing months that I was with this project I observed the emergence of a highly effective team that exhibited a mission driven, collaborative ethos.

Premises Underlying this Book

This section of the introductory chapter identifies the book's major premises. Each of the premises is addressed in some detail in the remaining chapters of the book.

- Collaborative organizations differ from stand-alone organizations that have hierarchical structures with a single person at their apex. Collaborative organizations are not bureaucratic, top down organizations. In fact, they are bottom up organizations and often have multiple, horizontal relationships. Readers of this book will come to understand the characteristics of collaborative organizations and the leadership challenges they pose.

- Research and Development organizations are collaborative organizations; they provide useful insights into behaviors and attributes of leaders that are compatible with the requisites of inter-sectoral collaborative organizations. Technical Directors of Laboratories and managers of their programs and projects lead without relying on bureaucratic authority; yet they are able to carry out their leadership responsibilities effectively. These individuals lead by example, earn respect for their expertise, gain trust by being trustworthy, and are adept at influencing and persuading their followers to commit their talents and energy to shared goals and values. Chapter 8 goes into more detail on this premise.

- It is useful to revisit quality literature on leadership to glean insights from that literature that are particularly well suited for use by collaborative leaders.

- Leaders of collaborative organizations need to be well grounded in organizational theories and organizational analysis. These leaders need to have a "bag of conceptual tools and techniques" to assist them in steering their "fluid organizations".

- An ability to "frame" and "reframe" situations by viewing them through differing conceptual frames of reference and thereby guide organizational dynamics will be a particularly important attribute of collaborative leaders.

- "Leadership languages" will be beneficial assets in the context of collaborative organizations. These languages are composed of the many concepts, models, theories, metaphors and analogies leaders may choose to employ.

- Leadership approaches grounded in "systems thinking" will prove particularly useful to collaborative leaders. System thinking is grounded in a vast literature about differing facets of systems and the applications of systems concepts to challenges leaders face.

- Collaborative leaders need to skillfully nurture new ideas and technologies if they are to be successful in guiding the inventive and innovative efforts of their organizations.

Organization of the Remainder of Book

Today, we are seeing increasing numbers of inter-sectoral collaborative organizations—those that involve participation by organizations from at least two of three sectors; that is, the private, public, and not-for-profit. In Chapter 2, the characteristics of these collaborative organizations are identified and challenges facing leaders are discussed.

In Chapter 3, I delve into the leadership challenges that flow from the characteristics of collaborative organizations identified in Chapter

2. I do this by exploring what I consider to be among the best books on leadership for relevant insights. I mention only a few of the most relevant insights of each book and hope that some readers will be stimulated by these insights to obtain and read the entire book.

There are an enormous number of books on leadership. In the on-line class that, Paul Danczyk and I taught, sixty-five students were asked to summarize a book of their choice on leadership. There was very little overlap in their choices with the exception of *The Prince* by Machiavelli! The leadership books I have selected have all been written within the last one-hundred years. *The Principles of Scientific Management* by Frederick Winslow Taylor was published in the 1916. The most recent, The Contrarian's Guide to Leadership, by Steven Sample was published in 2002. I believe each of these books makes major contributions to our understanding of the art of leadership and has relevance for leaders of collaborative organizations.

Leadership "tools and techniques" are discussed in Chapter 4. This chapter focuses upon maps, models, theories and typologies. These conceptual tools will be defined and illustrated. The importance of the analogies and metaphors leaders employ will be discussed. Leaders are challenged to consider "what is in their "tool bag"? There are an enormous number of tools and techniques available to leaders, but which of those tools do they "own" and use in practice? This chapter seeks to assist leaders in reflecting on that question and in considering how they might augment their "tool bags"!

Chapter 5 differentiates preceptive and receptive thinking, and explores examples of lens and frames that are now part of the "accepted wisdom" that has currency with many leaders. Some of the works of major contributors to that body of wisdom will be singled out and examined in this chapter.

Two specific tools that are often overlooked in writings on leadership will be described and illustrated in Chapter 6. The first tool, system diagramming, flows out of a rich body of literature on system thinking. Industrial Engineers refined early efforts at systems and procedures analysis while constructing a raft of tools associated with Management Science and Operations Research. Economists, using a systems frame of reference, developed Systems Analysis as a means of weighing the costs and benefits of alternative system configurations. Systems Diagrams as described in this chapter, provide leaders with a gestalt for thinking of their organizations as "open systems".

Co-alignment analysis is the other system-based tool that can be of great value to leaders as they weigh their options for actions to keep their organizations in "harmony" with rapidly changing contextual factors. This tool can assist leaders in identifying their organization's "non-alignments" that will need to be resolved, and suggest possible options for bringing things back into alignment. Both of the above Systems-based models/tools are constructed using sets of language for analysis that are easily learned and can readily be added to one's tool bag.

The relationship between language and leadership is explored in Chapter 7. A leader's "language" includes the terminology and concepts he or she employs to think, speak, write and act regarding their particular collaborative organization and its people, policies, values etc. Their language shapes how leaders perceive problems and opportunities confronting them and/or their organizations. Much depends upon their language; it may clarify, cloud, or simplify the realities of their context. Often, where leaders stand on important issues, depends on their leadership language. In this chapter I will discuss a classic book on Role Theory to introduce readers to a valuable language for Role analysis.

Chapter 8 provides a case study of an exemplary Research and Development leader, Dr. William B. McLean, the inventor/innovator of the Sidewinder missile. The two Navy Laboratories that Dr. McLean led had hundreds of ongoing projects and project teams that normally worked in non-hierarchical settings in collaboration with private sector organizations and other government laboratories and agencies. This chapter begins with an explanation of three interrelated processes: ideation, invention and innovation. It next discusses a typology for classifying organizations based upon their degree of innovativeness. This material provides a useful backdrop for telling the story of Dr. McLean and his Sidewinder missile and how its invention impacted the nation of Taiwan.

A brief concluding chapter is provided at the end of the book; it summarizes some of the principal ideas contained in the book.

Following the Conclusion is an Appendix which provides guidance and principles for developing a common form of collaborative organization, a public, private partnership. The Appendix reflects the rich experience base with this form of collaborative arrangement on the part of its author, John Shirey, who is a nationally renowned City Manager. John is presently the City Manager of Sacramento, California.

Chapter 2

Characteristics and Leadership Challenges of Collaborative Organizations

Background

Collaborative Organizations come in many different forms. For example, they may be temporary organizations that are formed based on **mutual aid agreements**. When Fire and Police Departments experience critical incidents such as major fires or riots, they receive assistance from many other organizations based on these agreements. Once the incident is resolved, these temporarily assembled organizations cease to exist until the next incident. Ongoing joint task forces also are common collaborative arrangements. The Joint Crime Task Force for the Boston region reflected well on the potential of this form of partnership when the Boston Marathon terrorist incident occurred.

A more enduring collaboration may be a **public private partnership** that is formed to pursue objectives that a single organization is not able to take on. A current example is the City of Sacramento's partnering with the new owners of its NBA team to build and operate a modern sports arena. Other forms of collaboration include: **contractual arrangements** such as used by the Defense Department to engage the services of the Black-Water Corporation in Iraq; **market mechanisms** such as California has created to buy and sell "pollution rights" and thereby better control air pollution; and **networks** such as those that have been developed to share intelligence related to our anti-terrorism efforts within this country and around the world.*

Articles addressing some of these forms of collaborative organizations are listed here for readers with an interest in a particular type of collaborative arrangement. Public Private Partnerships are addressed in the Appendix of this book by John Shirey, City Manager of Sacramento. For collaborations via contracts, I recommend, "A Contractual Framework for New Public Management Theory," by James Ferris and Elizabeth A. Graddy which appears in the *International Public Management Journal*, vol.1 no.2 (1998): pp. 225-240. For market based collaborative arrangements, I recommend, "Los Angeles's Clean Air Saga—Spanning the Three Epochs," by Daniel A. Mazmanian-published in 2008 *in Toward Sustainable Communities*, D. Mazmanian and M. Kraft, Editors.

In this chapter we address the question, what are some of the **characteristics** of collaborative organizations? We do not claim that we have created an exhaustive list of these characteristics but do believe we have pointed out some of the more important ones. Then, for each characteristic, we briefly examine some of the **leadership challenges** that these characteristics pose. In Chapter 3 we go into these challenges in more depth revisiting some of the classic writings on leadership to discern what insights they contain that can assist collaborative leaders in meeting the identified challenges. Subsequent chapters also address some of the major leadership challenges in considerable depth.

Characteristics and Leadership Challenges of Collaborative Organizations

In this section some characteristics of collaborative organizations are identified. The leadership challenges which flow from these characteristics are noted. Many of these insights came into focus while I was reading and grading papers written by fifty-five graduate students who were taking classes on Inter-Sectoral Leadership from the University of Southern California's Price School of Public Policy. These students wrote papers on a wide variety of collaborative organizations from around the world.

Characteristics of Collaborative organizations and the leadership challenges they pose are identified and discussed below:

- **Supportive Relationships:** Collaborative organizations have to build and maintain supportive relationships with their "parent" organizations if they are to be successful.

The leadership challenge is to learn how to attain a degree of autonomy for their collaborative organization while building mutual trust and respect with their "parent organizations" and acquiring their ongoing support?

- **Loyalty:** Participants in collaborative organizations have **multiple loyalties**—to the collaborative organization, to their parent organizations and to their own careers.

The challenge is to help employees sort through potential conflicting loyalties and assist them in developing a set of "multiple loyalties" between participants and the collaborative and parent organizations.

- **Hierarchy:** Collaborative organizations are **non-hierarchical**; power is widely dispersed.

Challenges this characteristic creates for leaders include: In the absence of a single authority, how do you effectively wield influence? How do decisions get made? How are conflicts resolved? How are rewards and punishments dispensed? And who sets priorities in terms of time, cost and performance objectives?

- **Resource acquisition:** In their early stages, collaborative organizations often have difficulty obtaining start-up resources and later, attaining stable long run financial and human resources.

The challenge for leaders is to learn how to ensure continuing access to financial and human resources for their collaborative organization. Having-well honed "political skills" will be crucial.

Lewis Apartment Communities

New Year, New Neighbors!
Refer family or friends
and receive $$$ for your referral!

ᴴᴵᴾ 95835

UTILITIES BILL

Homecoming at
Creekside
4800 Kokomo Drive
Sacramento, CA 95835
916-419-0995

RETURN SERVICE
REQUESTED

USAGE PERIOD	DUE DATE	# OCCUPANTS
12/1/2018 - 12/31/2018	2/1/2019	1

BILLING DATE	ᴺᵁᴵᵀᴵ	
1/7/2019		

ACCOUNT NUMBER	UNIT NUMBER	AMOUNT DUE
3129225-240	6121	$71.34

PLEASE PAY WITH RENT

DESCRIPTION	AMOUNT
WATER	$8.06
USAGE (curr - prev)	
(6257 - 6149) 108	
SEWER	$53.29
TRASH	$6.94
TRASH ADMIN FEE	$0.50
SERVICE FEE	$2.55
AMOUNT DUE	**$71.34**

THIS BILL IS DUE ON THE 1ST AND WILL BE LATE AFTER THE 5TH

PLEASE PAY WITH RENT
MAKE PAYMENT TO LEWIS MANAGEMENT CORP.

WHEN KWON
4851 KOKOMO DR APT 6121
SACRAMENTO CA 95835-1843

- **Group Problem Solving**: An ability to solve problems is critical to collaborative undertakings since by definition, these organizations involve individuals from two or more organizations seeking to collaborate; they will have work through the many differences that flow out of their having come out of multiple organizations that have different histories, systems and procedures, and value and belief systems.

The challenge for leaders is to identify and adopt group problem solving techniques such as Paul Buchanan's approach to group problem solving (published by Leadership Resources, Inc.) and Kepner and Tregoe's book, *The Rational Manager*, which addresses problem analysis, decision analysis and potential problem analysis. Leaders will have to convince participants in their collaborative ventures to invest their time and energy to learn these or other techniques and use them effectively to arrive at problem solutions.

- **Conflict**: Differences are to be expected; bargaining, negotiation and consensus-building skills are critical.

The challenge for leaders is to facilitate training and development of their collaborative organization's members in these areas, and to guide their efforts in applying these skills in the ongoing work of their organization.

- **Trust**: This is an essential element in collaborative organizations.

The challenge for leaders is to learn to model trustworthy behavior in their own actions and to recognize and reward organizational members whose behaviors demonstrate their trustworthiness.

- **Role Conflict and Ambiguity**: In the early stages of collaborative efforts, both individual and organizational **roles are ambiguous**; there is a lack of clarity regarding what expectations should or should not be held for participating individuals and organizations.

The challenge for leaders is to work through ambiguous and or conflicting expectations, clarify those expectations, and build "expectation consensus" and an understanding of these roles.

- **Risk-Taking:** This characteristic of these organizations stems from their origination, which is often as an experiment; collaborative organizations contain individuals and have organizational "parents" who have demonstrated a willingness to take risks and capitalize on "emergent opportunities". These organizations tend to be entrepreneurial, not traditional bureaucracies.

Leaders are challenged to create a culture that is congruent with their being an innovative organization. (I argue that the literature on, and practices of Research and Development organizations, are instructive for collaborative leaders interested in nurturing innovative behavior).

- **Fluidity:** Collaborative organizations are dynamic! Their members often wear several hats and may continue to have one foot in a parental organization, and the other in the collaborative organization. Some members will be on short term assignments; others may be full-time for many years. These organizations often operate horizontally across their boundaries with many other organizations within interdependent, shifting networks. The goals and objectives of collaborative organizations will change over time and their environments will be in constant flux.

The leadership challenges that flow from this characteristic are numerous. Developing a capacity for "system thinking" will be crucial to successfully leading these organizations. Similarly, the ability to learn from experiences and work within network contexts will be of paramount importance. System thinking is the subject of chapter 6 below. Working within networks is quite important. This will also be discussed in Chapter 6. An article on this topic that I recommend for readers is, "Do Networks Really Work: A Framework for Evaluating Public Sector Organizational Networks," by Keith Provan and Brinton

Milward. This article appears in the *Public Administration Review,* Vol. 61, No. 4., (2001): pp. 414-423.

Chapter 2 has identified some of the characteristics that are inherent in collaborative organizations and then pointed to the leadership challenges these characteristics pose. These leadership challenges will be discussed in the next chapter. It should be noted that some challenges such as role conflict and ambiguity, and fluidity are addressed by entire chapters later in the book.

Chapter 3

Leadership Literature

This chapter will examine some of the best leadership literature written over the years. The intent is to pull out from these sources useful insights when it comes to meeting the leadership challenges that flow from the characteristics of collaborative organizations as identified in the preceding chapter. The chosen authors have presented a multitude of useful insights in their books. Admittedly, I touch on only a few of their many contributions. For instance, Warren Bennis has published 27 books to date related to leadership! My hope is that the ideas that they presented prove useful to leaders of collaborative organizations, and that readers will wish to read more of their published works.

Landmark Leadership Authors

At the outset of this section, let me acknowledge that there has been much written related to the subject of leadership for more than two thousand years. Writers such as Socrates, Leonardo da Vinci, and Nicolai Machiavelli, are notable for their contributions to this topic. However, I am choosing to focus upon the last one hundred years. Authors I have selected from the early half of the twentieth century include: Frederick Winslow Taylor, Mary Parker Follett, Chester Barnard, John Gardner, Richard Neustadt, Donald Schon, Warren Bennis and Steven Sample. In addition to exploring these Landmark figures, other writers will be mentioned more briefly in this chapter, as will a few recent articles.

Frederick W. Taylor

Frederick W. Taylor in his 1916 book, *The Principles of Scientific Management*, sought to improve the efficiency of worker performance by developing a "scientific" body of knowledge that could be taught to workers to improve their productivity in areas such as metal cutting, shoveling, etc. Leaders (often foremen in this instance) were "teachers" of their workers. Taylor's premise was that by teaching them the "one best way" to perform a task, productivity could be increased and workers would benefit by receiving higher wages.

One of the more interesting ideas Taylor advanced was labeled "functional foremanship". In this scheme, workers would have eight foremen guiding their work; they would have multiple planning foremen and multiple operational foremen who would assist them in being as productive as possible. It could be said that each worker had eight leaders, which definitely conflicted with Max Weber's theory of bureaucracy published in 1922 in his book *Economy and Society* and Luther Gulick's belief in "structures of authority" and "principles of management" as reflected in his co-edited book, *Papers on the Science of Administration* published in 1937.

One of Gulick's fundamental principles of management was that a "unity of command" must exist under which each employee had a direct reporting relationship to a single authority figure. Taylor's view of functional foremanship emphasized the importance of knowledge and technical expertise as requisites for leadership rather than having positional authority in a "command and control" hierarchy. Taylor's view was largely dismissed in his own time, but having multiple leaders has more resonance today when increasingly **knowledge and expertise are bases for influence** in organizations, and they are particularly important in collaborative organizations with their more fluid structures.

Mary Parker Follett

Mary Parker Follett is the author of several books and many thoughtful papers which were collected posthumously into a book, *Dynamic Administration*, edited by H.C. Metcalf and L. Urwick. Ms. Follett was initially a social worker and later, a management consultant to industrial and not-for profit leaders. Follett wrote numerous papers in the 1920s and 1930s that have relevance for leading today's collaborative organizations.

Ms. Follett was one of the early pioneers in the Human Relations movement, and is said to have coined such well known terms as "transformational leadership" and "win-win" solutions. She saw organizations as social systems. Follett's impact on her contemporaries such as Elton Mayo and Chester Barnard, and on subsequent human relations writers and consultants has been quite enormous.

Some of Follett's insights that are useful for leaders of collaborative organizations will be noted and discussed below.

In one of her papers, "The Giving of Orders", Follett advocated broad participation in studying the facts of a given situation to determine what should be done. Her view was that giving orders should be depersonalized and replaced by the "Law of the Situation". To her, "fact power" was the critical element in addressing situations and determining actions to be undertaken. If alive today, I am confident that Mary would urge leaders of collaborative organizations to foster **wide participation** in identifying situational facts and actions to be undertaken.

Follett was quite aware of the significance of informal organizations that operate within formal organizations. She was skeptical of vertical authority and spoke of leaders needing to think not of having "power over" their subordinates but rather of having "power with" them. As a student of our democratic institutions, she spoke of the importance of the consent of the governed within organizations.

Follett's view of power and influence was that they did not flow from formal authority as much as they did from interpersonal relationships and from individuals' areas of expertise. Follett also stressed the power of the goals of leaders and followers; she described goals as the organization's "invisible leaders", and she emphasized the value of having a sense of "common purpose".

Follett's view of conflict was that it could be reduced or eliminated if people sought out "integrated solutions" (win-win). She pointed out the flaws of resolving conflicts through domination or compromise and urged individuals to explore the facts of the situation in searching for a unifying solution. Follett believed that in conflict situations, "fact power" should be more influential than "people power". A governing assumption in collaborative undertakings needs to be that the interests of individual workers and multiple organizations are not mutually exclusive; win-win outcomes are to be valued and sought.

(A useful article by Albie M. Davis expands on Follett's views on conflict. That article is, "In Theory: An Interview with Mary Parker Follett," *Negotiation Journal*, (July 1989): pp.223-235.)

Building mutual loyalty requires consistent effort by all parties. Value congruence among individual employees and collaborative and parent organizations can be sought in the same ways that organizational cultures are formed; that is through symbolic acts, construction of myths, storytelling etc.

Chester Barnard

Chester Barnard was a leader in the private and not-for-profit sectors; he was President of the New Jersey Bell Telephone Company and later, President of the Rockefeller Foundation. Barnard's classic book, *The Functions of the Executive*, was first published in 1938; it became and still is a staple in Business School programs around the world.

Barnard was one of the first to conceive of organizations as "cooperative systems". The principal **functions** of executives which he derived from his systems conception are: establishing and maintaining a system of communication, securing essential services from organizational members, and formulating organizational purposes and objectives.

Barnard's views on authority are consistent with Mary Parker Follett's belief in the consent of the governed as an organizational principle. Barnard advanced an "acceptance theory of authority"; he argues that ultimately it is up to subordinates to accept whether a communication is authoritative or not.

Barnard's definition of effectiveness related it to the degree of goal accomplishment; however, his definition of efficiency was quite different. Barnard defined efficiency as the ability to satisfy the motives of the organization's members! His view was that managers need to treat their subordinates with respect and competence.

Barnard was among the first to write about intuition in leadership and management, and the limits to rational approaches. In his book, Barnard devoted a sizable appendix, "Mind in Everyday Affairs," to what he called, non-logical mental processes. These processes appear to be similar to what John Gardner (below) refers to as "judgment in action", and Donald Schon's suggestion (below) that leaders need to act before they know. Schon points to the limits of rational analytic processes to justify his suggestion. Barnard's appendix appears to have affected the thinking of other subsequent writers on leadership and management.

John Gardner

John Gardner's book, On Leadership, published in 1990, helps place the importance of leadership in organizations into perspective. Gardner acknowledges how important it is for organizations to have effective leaders. I am confident he would say that this is particularly true for collaborative organizations with their unique characteristics as discussed earlier. Nonetheless, Gardner indicates that leadership is only one of the factors impacting organizational success. Gardner points to the equal importance of having resources available, a workforce with high morale, and organizational social cohesion. Gardner goes on to say that organizations not only need effective leaders; they also need individuals who are innovators, entrepreneurs and thinkers.

Gardner has an insightful listing of the tasks of leadership in his book. His list includes:

- Envisioning goals

- Affirming values

- Regenerating values

- Motivating

- Managing

- Achieving social cohesion

- Preserving a level of trust

- Teaching and clarifying

- Serving as a symbol

- Representing the organization

- Guiding organizational renewal

Leaders of collaborative organizations must address the above tasks; in addition, they must pay particular attention to questions/issues of power and influence given the absence of a clear hierarchy.

Some of the characteristics of effective leaders that Gardner identifies are that they: think longer term; grasp relationships between their unit and larger realities; reason intuitively and make "judgments-in action" that subsequent events prove sound.

A couple of my favorite quotes from this Gardner book are: "How do you earn trust? Try being trustworthy!", and "Executives are given subordinates but they have to earn followers!"

In another of his books, *Self Renewal: The Individual and the Innovative Society*, John Gardner addresses the need for ever-renewing, innovative societies which he asserts to be dependent on having ever-renewing individuals. Gardner also has much to say about organizations; he provides rich insights into such matters as "organizational aging" and organizational "dry rot". His underlying premise in *Self Renewal* is that to avoid the pathologies of aging, individuals, organizations and societies need to work to be "ever renewing".

In *Self Renewal* Gardner employs organismic analogies and draws comparisons between maturation processes of individuals and organizations. He also uses metaphors based on gardening to explain how societies and organizations can be simultaneously decaying and bringing forth new life (seedlings). It is in this context that Gardner emphasizes the need for innovation and continuous change. Leaders in collaborative organizations should take note of Gardner's metaphor of the garden and keep careful watch on their organizations to ensure that any decay is offset by strategies to keep their organization youthful.

As collaborative leaders, you also need to be concerned about yourself. What are your strategies for self-renewal? There are plenty of options to consider. Collaborative leaders can participate in networks of peers leading similar or related organizations; participate in professional associations, enroll in education and training classes, read relevant books and articles, surf the net, and affiliate themselves with University faculty who share their areas of interest.

Richard Neustadt

Richard E. Neustadt was a Professor of Government at Columbia University in 1960, and a Special Consultant to President-Elect Kennedy. Neustadt wrote his book, *Presidential Power*, during and shortly after the Presidential transition. This classic book has been described as a primer for Presidents. The main focus of the book is, "personal power: how to get it, keep it and use it."

While Neustadt's book was written at Simon's "institutional layer", it is not much of a stretch to view it as equally relevant at the "organizational layer" as it contains valuable insights for leaders, and perhaps for particularly collaborative organization leaders who, like Presidents, do not have a hierarchical relationship with other organizations (institutions) upon which they are dependent. Simon's Map of our "Layered Society" will be briefly discussed in chapter 4. Basically, Simon views society as being composed of individual, group, organizational and institutional layers. Simon suggests that theories originated for one layer may have utility at other layers. Neustadt's advice to Presidents applies as well to organizational leaders as it does for leaders of nations.

Neustadt draws a clear distinction between powers and power; he equates "powers" to having formal authority, and "power" to your ability to influence others.

Neustadt refers to the vantage points you have in the play of power in and around your organization; he calls those vantage points your "power stakes". Two important power stakes he points to are your "professional reputation" and your "public prestige".

Neustadt defines "professional reputation" as "The judgment of those you wish to persuade as to your skill and willingness to use your vantage points". He goes on to define "public prestige" as "Your public (organizational) standing; that is how other actors anticipate the relevant "public" will react to those who oppose or support you."

Collaborative organizational leaders must realize that they need to be concerned about their "power image" in the organization and attempt to enhance it over time to increase their influence. Neustadt suggests that one's image is influenced by how you behave in handling important decisions—what he calls your "power laden choices"; that is, those decisions which will impact your professional reputation and public prestige. Wise collaborative leaders will be sensitive to their need to manage their image to increase their ability to influence those around them.*

*Let me recommend two related articles that contain useful insights for leaders interested in this topic. The first is "The Political Dimension of Effective Nonprofit Executive Leadership," by Richard D. Heimovics, et. al.; this article appeared in the Journal, *Nonprofit Management and Leadership* in the spring of 1995. The second article is "How to do (or not do) a Stakeholder Analysis," by Zsuzsa Varvasovszky and Ruari Brucha which appeared in *Health Policy and Planning* in vol. 15-3 (September 2000): pp. 338-345.

Donald Schon

Donald Schon was a Professor of Urban Studies and Education at the Massachusetts Institute of Technology. Schon is known for his contributions to the Planning Profession, to our understanding of how professionals combine reflection and action, and for his insights into the importance of learning as it relates to coping with continuous change. His remarkable book, *Beyond the Stable State*, offers many insights for leaders working in turbulent contexts. I touch upon only a few points of the arguments he advances in this book which is contained in the Bibliography.

The problem his book addresses is, "the rapidly accelerating rate of change that is undermining our society". Schon argues that we no longer live in a "Stable State," and proposes that our institutions must be "learning systems". His suggestion seems to fit the fluidity of collaborative organizations well. Some of the characteristics of learning systems that fit collaborative arrangements are:

- They maintain flexibility to adapt to situations as they arise
- They decentralize control
- They listen to incoming messages
- They act before they know

Judging from my reading of his book, some of the advice Schon would probably offer collaborative leaders follows:

- Be secure in situations of uncertainty
- As a "learning agent" for your organization, be willing and able to be an "informational instrument"
- Suspend your prior views, listen, confront and act
- Learn from your actions and their consequences
- Use your beliefs and values as your way of looking at the world
- Engage with others, but ultimately, rely on yourself

In another of his books, *The Reflective Practitioner: How Professionals Think in Action*, Schon provides many insights into the thought processes of leaders and adds to John Gardner's earlier noted observations on leaders needing to make "judgments in action". Schon asserts his view that professionals must act before they know! He sees major limits to rational analytical approaches and believes that "Reflective Practitioners" distill insights from their experiences and rely heavily on their intuitive reasoning. (A classic article that presents an argument that reinforces both Gardner's and Schon's views on the importance of judgment in action and intuitive reasoning is Charles Lindblom's, "The Science of Muddling Through," which appeared in the *Public Administration Review* in 1959.)

Warren Bennis

Warren Bennis has written approximately 30 books on leadership including the classic, *On Becoming a Leader*. A recent collection of his essays, *The Essential Bennis,* contains many of his leadership contributions. I have chosen to note here only two of his many insights into leaders and leadership that I have found particularly valuable, his definition of leaders and his list of core leadership competencies.

Bennis contrasts leaders and managers by asserting, "Leaders are people who do the right things; managers are people who do things right! Both roles are crucial, but they differ profoundly!" What I find very useful in this quote is that it reminds us all how important it is for leaders as well as followers to be habitually asking, are we doing the right things? What a terribly important question, particularly given ongoing changes in organizational environments. Leaders, managers and followers must be concerned about doing things right, but to do so while doing the wrong things is inexcusable.

Another insightful contribution of Bennis flows from his research on 90 successful leaders; he identifies four competencies evident in all the CEOs in his research sample. That these **competencies** apply to leaders of collaborative organizations appears to me to have "face validity".

- **Management of Attention**—provide a compelling vision for the organization. This competency provides an "invisible guide" for employees as they prioritize scarce resources such as use of their time.

- **Management of Meaning**—communicate your interpretation of events—leaders' interpretations of cardinal events affecting their organizations can have hugely positive impacts on their organizations' employee morale and social cohesion. An important role of leaders is to help organizational members understand ever changing organizational realities.

- **Management of Trust**—the main determinant of trust is a leader's reliability. Is he or she trustworthy?

- **Management of Self**—knowing one's skills and deploying them effectively. Take some time to think through your strengths and weaknesses; build on your strengths and find ways to compensate for your weaknesses.

Warren Bennis is widely admired; his books are enjoyable to read. I highly recommend reading books by Bennis for inspiration and insights. The final book to be noted in this chapter, *The Contrarian's Guide to Leadership*, is a "Warren Bennis Book"; it is one of a short list of fine books in Warren's signature series. Warren Bennis is the editor of a series of books on leadership that have been published by John Wiley and sons.

Steven Sample

Steven B. Sample's book, the *Contrarian's Guide to Leadership*, will prove particularly useful to senior level executives with significant collaborative leadership responsibilities. Dr. Sample was an exemplary leader as the 10th President of the University of Southern California; he previously had served as President of a public university, the State University of New York-Buffalo.

Sample's definition of, "a contrarian leader—one who sees situations from his own unique point of view and who finds genuinely new solutions to the problems facing his organization," is reflective of his own leadership practices. His book presents many of the lessons he learned from his own personal experiences as a thoughtful and effective leader.

Along with his many provocative insights Sample conveys a clear, fundamental message; namely, that leadership is an art and that leaders are always works in progress.

I will mention only three of Sample's many leadership suggestions:

> "Bring your natural creativity and intellectual independence to the fore."

"Listen first; talk later . . . . listen attentively without rushing to judgment."

"Never make a decision yourself that can reasonably be delegated to a lieutenant; and never make a decision today that can reasonably be put off until tomorrow."

Sample provides rich discussions of each of his 15 Contrarian leadership principles and illustrates them with experience based examples. Sample's book is an excellent "read"; I recommend it highly.

In Chapter 4 which follows, we shift to a discussion of the conceptual tools leaders can employ to increase their effectiveness.

Chapter 4

Leader's Conceptual Tools

One purpose of this book is to stimulate its readers to reflect upon their capacity as leaders throughout their careers. That is, how can they attain and then retain their ability to perform as leaders in the rapidly changing organizational and societal contexts present in the world today? Effective leaders require a commitment to a lifetime of effort to grow in their capacities to perform their leadership roles. This will require leaders to be reflective about their daily experiences as leaders; and to be open to fresh insights that can be gleaned from their reflections, from their interactions with others, and from reading and participating in experiential opportunities as they arise.

A premise underlying the book is that among the many requisites for performing leadership roles are: being knowledgeable regarding human behavior, particularly in organizational contexts; having a sound grasp of organizational and managerial theories and their strengths and limits; and being skilled in the use of "the conceptual tools of leadership" which include: maps, models, theories, concepts and frames of reference such as typologies, metaphors, analogies, and analytical languages. These tools are the subject of this chapter. Each of these tools will be defined and illustrated with examples. It should not take readers long to grasp these tools and begin to recognize their use both in books on leadership, organizational analysis and managerial behavior, and from their use in practice by artful leaders.

Maps, Models and Theories

Travelers make use of Maps (and GPS technology) to plan their trips and to sharpen their sense of the territory along their planned routes.

Maps and their accompaniments also provide them with insights into possibilities en route: interesting places to visit, optional paths to follow, priorities they may wish to establish etc. Leaders also need maps to better understand the body of knowledge available to assist them with their leadership responsibilities for goal setting, choosing a leadership style, deciding on organizational arrangements, building their organization's culture, creating human resource policies and philosophy, etc. Maps help provide a Gestalt, a broad sense of the body of knowledge available in the many areas of interest to leaders.

Maps help one to categorize this body of knowledge in various ways. For example, one map divides organization and management literature into Classical, Neo-Classical and Modern categories. Bolman and Deal's book, *Reframing Organizations*, classifies this same knowledge base into a map composed of four "frames"; that is, the Structural, Human Resources, Symbolic, and Political frames. These authors define frames as follows, "a frame is a mental model—a set of ideas and assumptions—that you carry in your head to help your understand and negotiate a particular 'territory.' A good frame makes it easier for you to know what you are up against and, ultimately, what you can do about it. Frames are vital because organizations don't come with computerized navigation systems to guide you turn by turn to your destination. Instead, managers need to develop and carry accurate maps in their head."

Herbert Simon, a Nobel-prize winner, provides us one of the most well-known maps of knowledge emanating from the Social Sciences that has relevance for leaders. Simon's scholarly work ranges broadly. His book, *Administrative Behavior*, is a classic; it contains his discussion of bounded rationality and satisficing which greatly impacted subsequent management theories. Simon is also noted for his scholarly work on Societal Complexity.

In his map, Simon conceives of society as being layered; the first column of his map shows his suggested layers; i.e., individual, role, group, organization, institution, and society as a whole. The second column of his map indicates which academic discipline has played a primary role in building the knowledge base regarding that layer;

for example, Psychology at the individual layer and Sociology at the group layer. Some layers such as the organizational layer are addressed by multiple disciplines and are interdisciplinary. The third column of Simon's Map identifies examples of bodies of theory that have been constructed for particular layers.

When asked which layers of Simon's map are particularly important to leaders or students preparing for leadership roles, it takes but a moment for leaders and students to conclude that all of the layers are important. In a nutshell, this explains how challenging it is to become knowledgeable regarding leadership responsibilities. The map also is an excellent diagnostic tool. Leaders can use it to assess which layers they feel most comfortable with and which layers they will need to work on to improve their knowledge base. Similarly, leaders can use the Bolman and Deal map to assess which of the four frames they are most or least informed about.

Simon introduces us to the concept of displacement. By displacement he refers to taking models or theories developed at one layer of society and making use of those models and theories at another layer. Warren Bennis, as an example, promoted the utility of the metaphor, "organizational health." Bennis readily acknowledges that the criteria he suggests for judging an organization's health are similar to the criteria identified by Marie Jahoda in her discussion of (mentally) healthy individuals. In essence Bennis shifted theoretical insights related to personalities at the individual layer to a theory at the organizational layer.

Those displaced criteria for organizational health include: having a sense of identity-knowing who you are and what you are about; a clear perception of the realities of your context, the ability to adapt to a changing environment, the ability to cope with and solve problems, and the ability to self-regulate in the sense of being self-confident, self-reliant and self-accepting. Leaders of Collaborative Organizations will be wise if they apply these criteria in assessing the health of their organizations.

Concepts are the building blocks for models and theories. Concepts are nouns that give names to the shared characteristic of objects and events. Examples are: organizations, leaders, strategies, systems, and roles.

Models and Theories are constructed from sets of concepts; they are conceptual frames of reference for defining and organizing various organizational phenomena in order to facilitate thinking about them. Examples include the Systems Model discussed in detail in chapter 6 and Role Theory which is addressed in chapter 7. The term, theory, is used in different ways. Sometimes, a theory is simply a speculation. On other occasions it may be used normatively to assert that certain things should be done; for example, leaders should convey a sense of presence or should behave in their organization's best interest. Theories also may be descriptive and attempt to provide causal explanations for what is going on. In this book, my use of these terms is focused upon their use in aiding leaders to think about and better comprehend organizational phenomena.

Figure 1 below represents an example of a model that can aid leaders' thinking. The figure presents a generic model applicable to any organization. The model identifies the major variables present in all organizations and asserts that those variables are interdependent. That is, if you change any one of them, there are ripple effects on the others. The model is congruent with systems thinking as discussed in chapter 6. As leaders make changes in any of the organizational variables, they will be wise to think through the likely consequences for the other variables so that they can reinforce positive consequences and mitigate negative ones.

GENERIC ORGANIZATION MODEL
SEVEN INTERDEPENDENT VARIABLES

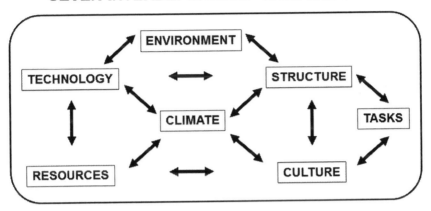

Other illustrations of models-theories contained in this book include; system diagrams, co-alignment models, role sets and role theory.

Models and theories have many useful functions; for example, they:

- Help leaders organize their thoughts and recall relevant past experiences
- Facilitate reasoning about organizational situations
- Suggest what questions should be asked and answered to improve one's understanding of what is going on
- Aid comparisons and contrasts between experiences
- Increase our perceptions and understanding of ongoing events

Metaphors and Analogies

Metaphors are figures of speech; two concepts are used in conjunction to convey an implied comparison between the concepts. For example, the metaphor, "scientific management" implies that there is a science underlying management. Supreme Court Justice Brandeis coined this metaphor which attempted to associate positive attitudes toward science with the work of Frederick Taylor aimed at increasing worker efficiency. This metaphor implies that management can be studied and a science of management can be produced if those studies are subjected to the rigorous standards associated with scientific studies.

Other examples of metaphors include: organizational health, bureaucratic imperialism, organizational aging, administrative iatrogenesis, and organizational chauvinism. Leaders often "salt" their speeches with metaphors to help their listeners more readily grasp their messages.

Analogies are used to compare organization and management phenomena with similar though not identical phenomena. For example, it is commonplace to associate organisms such as people, animals or plants with organizations. Organizations are described as going through phases of maturation; they are youthful, aging, senescent etc. Leadership is likened to steering a ship. Organizations are compared to machines, factories, sports teams, families etc. Similarly, governmental budgets are compared to personal budgets as though they are equivalents. Analogies may clarify or cloud realities; nonetheless they are used frequently by leaders.

Language employed by leaders is important. The concepts and models that you employ have powerful impacts upon what you see in situations, how you go about analyzing those situations, and take action; and how you communicate your analyses and actions to your subordinates, peers, super-ordinates and the various publics with which your organization interacts. An entire chapter, Chapter 7, is devoted to illustrating this point. An exceptionally useful language for role analysis is presented in that chapter. In Chapter 5 which follows additional leadership "thinking tools", lens, and frames, are discussed and illustrated.

Typologies

Typologies are multidimensional classification schemes to aid us in understanding organizational phenomena. One well known example is the Blake-Mouton Grid for classifying leadership styles. This typology calls for rating of leaders on ten point scales. One scale relates to the leader's concern for people; the other, their concern for productivity. When combined, the two ratings enable you place the rated leader on a grid. Style labels are attached to different locations on the grid to differentiate leaders; style labels might include Country Club Leaders or Task-oriented Bastards!

In chapter 8 in this book a typology is presented to differentiate and classify organizations based upon the point in time they choose to adopt and employ innovations that are coming into use within their organizational sets. Organizational adoptive practices regarding innovations are classified and labels are assigned that are descriptive of their behaviors.

Chapter 5

Thinking Tools: Lens and Frames

Leaders need to be self-conscious about their thinking skills and preferred modes of thinking. This chapter will first discuss receptive and preceptive thinking. Then, it will turn its focus to the range of thinking tools leaders can include in their professional repertoire.

Receptive Thinking and Logical Analysis

The term, receptive thinking, refers to a leader's capabilities in acquiring data and then logically analyzing that data to produce useful information. Leaders can be receptive to information by being effective listeners; by working with their network of contacts, by selective reading of reports, newspapers and journals, and by creating a culture that fosters openness to inputs from subordinates and peers. Obtaining negative feedback of information is not always easy, but it definitely helps if you have developed a reputation for not "shooting the messenger!"

Data acquired through receptive thinking channels requires analysis. Let's use the term, logical analysis, to refer to the processing of incoming data. A standard technique for logical analysis that I was first exposed to as a student at the University of California at Los Angeles called for a disciplined thought process. The technique requires that you first identify relevant "facts" important to a particular situation, and list them by number.

Next, you proceed to identify "conclusions" that can be logically inferred from the facts. Again you should number those conclusions. A required step in this form of analysis is to indicate for each "numbered conclusion" the facts that warrant that conclusion. The numbers for those facts should be shown adjacent to each conclusion. There should be no conclusions that are not derived from facts. Facts that are not shown as warranting any of your conclusions are probably not particularly important and can safely be dismissed from you analysis.

Finally, if the situation calls for coming up with recommended actions, those "recommendations" should be numbered. The conclusions that logically lead to each recommendation also should be identified by placing their numbers next to the recommendations they support.

This highly disciplined approach to processing available data makes the logic underlying your recommendations explicit and transparent. This approach is used by academics in their teaching; newspaper articles, case studies, and written reports can be scrutinized thoughtfully using this technique. Additionally, when you are the one generating reports, you can produce a very useful executive summary of your report by identifying the facts and conclusions that underlie the recommendations your report puts forth. Combining receptive thinking and logical analysis is quite useful for many of the situations leaders will periodically confront.

There are other techniques for aiding receptive thinking that leaders can readily master and employ. For example, Kepner and Tregoe in their book, *The Rational Manager*, outlined out an approach to problem identification and analysis which calls for finding (receiving) factual answers to a series of problem diagnostic questions such as, Who? What? When? Where? How? and, To What Extent is the problem occurring? Answers to these questions enable a leader to better understand a problem and its context.

Another receptive thinking technique which entails mass interviewing of people is the Crawford Slip Method. Professor Gilbert B. Siegel and I published a monograph on this method, *Mass Interviewing and the Marshaling of Ideas to Improve Performance: The Crawford Slip Method*.

Dr. C.C. Crawford developed his slip method during WW II to aid the military in their generation of manuals by systematically capturing the knowledge of numerous individuals regarding optimal procedures for work accomplishment. Fifty years later, near the time of his death, Dr. Crawford was still working with Air Force Colonels and Majors to re-write major Air Force procurement manuals. These knowledgeable officers assembled daily in the basement of Dr. Crawford's home in his "Think Tank".

Dr. Crawford considered meetings in which people spoke one at a time (and tended to ramble), a great waste of talent and energy. Instead, he worked to capture simultaneously the knowledge, ideas and insights of every individual in meetings. Each attendee was put to work writing slips, one idea at a time on carefully crafted "targets". Crawford had numerous clever techniques to keep ideas flowing. After these data gathering meetings, Crawford and perhaps an assistant or two would analyze the 2 and 3/4 by 4 and 1/4inch slips, organize them into coherent clusters and then feed the results back to the idea generators who were asked in a next iteration to further refine the results and write even more slips at ever increasing levels of detail.

Crawford's inductive approach to data gathering and his subsequent analyses produced literally thousands of manuals, reports, Masters' degree theses, and doctoral dissertations. Crawford personifies a receptive thinker; use of his slip method by staff and/or consultants can provide leaders with valuable information for use in their receptive thinking.

Preceptive Thinking

The term, preceptive thinking, refers to leaders' abilities to think deductively about their organizational situation by using models, theories, lens, and frames to order, filter, and make sense of information. Leaders who are "preceptive thinkers" often find themselves applying conceptual tools as thinking aids to gain insight into and an understanding of these situations.

Leaders need to be self-consciously aware of the extent to which they use lenses and models and what the strengths and weaknesses of these tools are. Experienced leaders are likely to be using many tools, at times intuitively. These tools aid them in their preceptive thinking. My intent in this section is to heighten readers' awareness of how they think about organizational realities. In the paragraphs that follow, I discuss and illustrate the utility of lens and frames as conceptual tools of leaders.

Lens

The term lens is often used interchangeably with the terms, theory and model; each is a tool for looking at organizational phenomena and interpreting their meaning.

John Pfiffner and Frank Sherwood published their book, *Administrative Organization*, in 1960. Important themes in their book are that organizations are complex, and that the "Concept of Overlays" represents one approach to understanding complex organizations. The story that has been shared over the years to explain the genesis of this concept is that John Pfiffner was teaching his class, making use of a series of transparencies which he projected onto a screen. In an absent-minded moment, John placed or "overlay" his next transparency upon one already on the projector. John's first transparency showed the hierarchical structure of an organization. His next transparency showed additional information about the organization in terms of who in the organization had power, regardless of their hierarchical position. These authors were quick to realize that by overlaying a series of transparencies dealing with such matters as who communicates with whom; what does the informal organization look like, who are social isolates or communication stars, who has power etc., produces a much fuller understanding of an organization and its dynamics. Each transparency essentially was providing a lens to improve one's vision of the organization.

Amitai Etzioni published an article in the *Public Administration Review* in 1967, "Mixed Scanning, A Third Approach," that suggested the utility of employing both broad angle and zoom lenses in approaching decision making. Etzioni contrasted his approach with rational and incremental approaches to decision making. His analogy for scanning was the way in which satellites make use of differing lenses for differing purposes. Etzioni in essence suggested that decision makers should first take a broad look at the landscape before selecting areas to zoom in on for a more detailed look. Etzioni's lenses provided a way leaders could first take a comprehensive look at problem situations and then selectively zoom in for more analytic detail before making a decision. In essence, he made the point that what you see depends upon both where and how you look, and that there are obvious limitations to both the rational and incremental approaches to decision making. We will come back to this point as we discuss framing and multi-framing below.

Frames

Lee Bolman and Terrence Deal published the fourth edition of their classic book, *Reframing Organizations*, in 2008. The sub-title of their book is *Artistry, Choice and Leadership*. These authors view leaders as artists who are adept at what they call multi-framing or the use of multiple lenses to view organizational situations. Their "map" of the literature on organizational and management theories includes four frames: the Structural, Human Resource, Political and Symbolic Frames.

Bolman and Deal define frames as mental models composed of a set of ideas and assumptions. The central theme of their book is that there is great merit for leaders to look at situations in their organizations in four different ways by "reframing" the situations using the four frames, which they then discuss in detail.

This is a book worthy of being on every leader's book shelf. Each of the four frames is made up of multiple concepts, models, typologies and theories. Clearly, there are many valuable leadership tools that are not covered in the Bolman and Deal book, but when combined, their frames provide a good start for leaders interested in filling their tool bags with concepts, models, theories, typologies, metaphors, and analogies.

Earlier we mentioned the limitations of rational and incremental approaches to decision making. The limits are explainable in part by the fact that lenses, models, theories and frames all produce partial pictures of organizational realities. These conceptual tools draw one's attention to sub-sets of all factors that exist, which affect an organization's performance and capacity to perform. This limitation can be offset to some degree by what Bolman and Deal refer to as "multi-framing". When they feel it necessary, leaders can overlay multiple lenses, frames and models to obtain a sharper grasp of what is going on in their organizations.

Leaders who understand the assumptions and component elements of the four frames around which Bolman and Deal focus their book will be well positioned to multi-frame. An additional frame, the Systems frame discussed in chapter 6, is also to be valued. Leaders interested in obtaining as clear an understanding of their organizations, both internally and externally, in terms of how well they are fitting in their ever changing contexts, require a well-rounded knowledge of organizational and management theories and a tool bag that includes multiple conceptual tools and analytical techniques.

In chapter 6 which follows, the systems frame is discussed in some depth; it provides readers with two useful tools, systems diagrams and co-alignment models.

Chapter 6

Systems Models for Leaders

In chapter 5 you were introduced to the "four frames" described and illustrated in Bolman and Deal's book, *Reframing Organizations*. In this chapter you will be provided information on a fifth frame, the "systems frame". First, background information is provided on the evolution of this frame of reference. This approach to managing and analyzing organizations has developed along numerous strands and continues to evolve.

After providing this backdrop information, two models that I believe will be particularly useful to leaders of collaborative organizations will be described and illustrated. The first of these models is a "Systems Diagram"; the second is a "Co-alignment Model". Both of these models help leaders develop a "gestalt" for thinking about their organizations. The models emphasize the ongoing exchanges between organizations and their environments. Both models start from the premise that collaborative organizations are "open systems" that are continuously importing and exporting information, goods, services etc. as they interact with other networks and organizations beyond their own boundaries.

Evolution of Systems Thinking

It is possible to trace the roots of systems thinking back to individuals such as Leonardo da Vinci, but I have chosen to identify, as the first "systems strand", the work of Frederick W. Taylor who has been called the "Father of Scientific Management". In the first two decades of the twentieth century, Taylor conducted systematic time and motion studies of work and workers; his intent was to increase efficiency in the workplace. His studies included helping the cement industry become more efficient in their use of manpower and materials; improving the efficiency of steel cutting by focusing upon man-machine relationships; and developing a "science of shoveling" by conducting studies to identify both the correct shovel size and shape for the material being shoveled, and the most efficient techniques for workers to employ in their shoveling.

Taylor's systematic studies produced a growing body of knowledge on these subjects; it was his work that underlay the initial experiments with lighting and worker productivity in the classic Hawthorne studies that contributed impetus to the Human Relations approach. The roots of Industrial Engineering include Taylor and his studies and this seminal systems strand. Similarly, the fields of Operations Research and Management Science are in his debt.

A second "systems strand", organizations as systems, came on the scene in the 1930's in the application of systems thinking and concepts to discussions of organizations. Chester Barnard in his classic book, *The Functions of the Executive*, devoted the first part of the book to what he called, "Systems of Cooperation". In this part he examined the individual in the organization, the physical and biological limitations in cooperative systems, and psychological and social factors in systems of cooperation. Barnard then went on to set out some "Principles of Cooperative Action". Barnard's seminal book stands out as perhaps the first holistic conception of organizations; he demonstrates the interdependence of personal, physical, biological, psychological and social factors and considers each to be important in attaining organizational efficiencies and effectiveness.

Program and Project management is a third strand in the evolution of system thinking. In this strand system thinking is applied to the organization and management of programs and projects. I am using the term, program, to describe complex undertakings that involve multiple projects. NASA's space programs and the Navy's Polaris program which encompassed multiple projects are illustrations. Project is the term commonly used to describe more focused efforts on a singular objective such as McLean's Sidewinder project. However, I recognize that these terms have been used in various ways by others. For example, the Manhattan Project led by Robert Oppenheimer and General Grove involved numerous organizations and projects, and could have been called the Manhattan Program.

Systems thinking underpins both program and project management in that there are program or project managers who are expected to grasp complex undertaking in their entirety. While program and project managers do not have unitary authority, they do have very substantial influence over their programs or projects as they are the "master architects" at the Center of the network of involved organizations and guide the flow of information and to some extent resources to the multiple subsystem leaders.

Project managers are in my mind useful comparison models for thinking about leaders of collaborative undertakings in the inter-sectoral context. Project managers can't rely upon hierarchical authority, so their ability to influence others resides primarily in their knowledge and understanding the project (system) as a whole and of its interdependent parts. Their challenge is to persuade other members of the project team that they should follow their lead because of their holistic grasp of the project.

An offshoot of concern over the management of projects and programs is the emergence of new system based planning and control techniques such as PERT—Program Evaluation and Review Technique—which was developed by Lockheed and Booz-Allen and Hamilton for the managers of the Polaris Missile Program. This network-based system for planning a project, and then monitoring and controlling the project's progress in carrying out the plan, has been widely used in the Defense, Space and Construction industries.

System Analysis for decision making is a fourth strand in the evolution of system thinking.
Roland McKeen was a pioneer in developing system analysis. His book, *Efficiency in Government Through Systems Analysis*, informed the decision making process with respect to River Systems. Professor

McKeen provided an early, insightful description and application of cost-benefit analysis to issues such as dam locations, sizes etc.

McKeen along with Charles Hitch produced a second path breaking book, *The Economics of Defense in a Nuclear Age*. This book advocated the use of cost-benefit and cost-effectiveness analyses in defense decision-making by carefully examining the trade-offs involved between weapon system options, when considered quite broadly. For example, is it more cost-effective to invest in a new aircraft carrier, a submarine, a joint services jet aircraft wing or manpower for limited warfare units? System analysts expanded the system boundaries within which options were to be considered. Alain Enthoven's book, *Systems Analysis*, provides an excellent overview of this strand. Secretary Robert McNamara fostered this approach as he insisted that he be given a broad array of decision options to select among.

Cybernetics represents a fifth strand in the evolution of system thinking; this strand relates to the use of systems concepts in control systems. Norbert Wiener, a mathematician working at MIT, first used the term cybernetics in his book, *Cybernetics,* to refer to control systems being developed for missiles. Cybernetics is derived from a Greek word that conveys the notion of steering. Very rapid electronic "feedback" is employed in missile control systems to stabilize and guide them in their flight.

The flow of information in organizations is equally critical to leaders attempting to steer them toward their goals and objectives. Evaluation research is often aimed at providing leaders with information for their steering decisions. Karl Deutsch provides us an insightful discussion of steering governments in his book, *The Nerves of Government*.

The current emphasis upon having information systems that provide accurate and timely information to organizational leaders reflects the influence of Wiener's work on Cybernetics.

"Functional Systems" are a sixth strand of system thinking that emerged in the 1970s. This strand focuses our attention on the evolution of systems, and the ability to modify their behavior as they "learn". This strand also helps us better understand how having "shared value commitments" can produce a dynamic of learning and collaboration that leads first to informal cooperation, and gradually to more formalized forms of cooperation through networks.

Donald Schon, in his book, *Beyond the Stable State*, directs our attention to "Functional Systems" which he describes as complex organizations which knit together a number of organizations or organizational elements into networks and make it possible for them to work in concert. Collaborative organizations fit the category of functional systems in some regards; they involve multiple organizations and they do not emphasize formal authority. Instead, they stress goal commitment, common values and rely on influence processes that emphasize knowledge and technical expertise.

According to Schon, Functional Systems often begin as informal shadow networks and gradually evolve into more formal networks of organizations working in concert. Among his illustrations of this evolution are the nutritional and blindness systems that started with minimal, not so visible collaboration, and have become recognized, interactive networks of groups and organizations that now work in concert on behalf of their clientele.

It is inevitable that over time, many collaborative organizations will become a part of Functional Systems that emerge first as shadow organizations and later as more formalized networks. According to James Thompson in his book, *Organizations in Action*, formal organization theories often put us in a conceptual box; they assume membership in single organizations with unitary authority structures. Thompson noted years ago that over time, many of us will participate in several organizations that place little emphasis on hierarchical authority.

In the closing sections of this chapter, two systems models which have great potential utility for leaders of collaborative organizations will be discussed and illustrated. Exercises that readers may perform are suggested to help them to add these two models to their personal tool bags.

The Systems Frame and System Diagrams

The Systems Frame is similar to the Bolman and Deal frames discussed in the previous chapter; this frame also has a set of underlying assumptions about organizations that are important to understand; namely, that:

- Organizations can usefully be thought of as organisms like cells, animals and humans.

- Organizational systems are composed of sets of interdependent units and the "flows" and relationships between these units.

- Linkages between the interdependent units is what forms systems.

- Systems must be grasped as a whole; thinking of them in terms of their parts is not sufficient.

- Models can be used to visualize systemic relations. The graphics below which show a systems diagram and a co-alignment model illustrate this point.

- Systems "nest"; they contain internal sub-systems and operate within more encompassing supra-systems. For example, one can think of cities and counties as subsystems of states and states as a part of a national-state supra-system. Similarly, universities are composed of schools and departments as sub-systems and they operate within a higher education supra-system.

As you have probably come to suspect by now, there is a "language" or set of concepts associated with the systems frame! That language will be set out for you in the discussion of the systems diagram. Figure 2 depicts a typical systems diagram. I will illustrate its use by applying the diagram to a non-profit organization. The University of Southern California and its Price School of Public Policy will be used as examples in the narrative description of a system which follows.

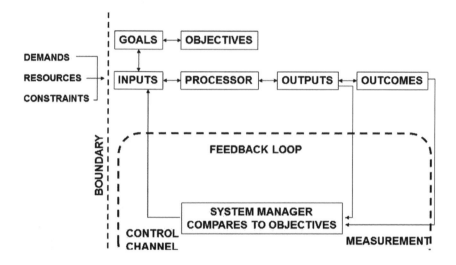

Processors can be thought of as entire organizations such as the University of Southern California, or as a part of USC's component sub-systems such as the Price School. For some purposes you can treat a processor as a "black box"; that is, you can simply observe the flow of inputs into the processor and the outputs that flow out of it. A processor is an input to output conversion mechanism; its efficacy can be observed without knowing what is going on inside the system. A commonly used illustration of the rationale for this approach asks, what is it that makes a dog wag its tail? It does not take an observer very long to identify the inputs that lead to the output of a tail wagging. One observer noted, dissecting the dog is not necessary, or for that matter, desirable.

Processors can also be micro-analyzed by examining each of their sub-systems and the flows between them. For example, one can trace the flow of students from their admission into the university until their graduation with a degree, and for some, their flow into graduate programs. Depending upon the level of detail desired for your look at a processor or processors, you can opt for the level of system information you require.

Inputs flow across systems' boundaries from their environments. Inputs into systems take the form of Demands, Constraints and Resources. Examples of Demands (Thou shalts) placed on USC are: accreditation standards, alumni and student demands, peer institutions expectations etc. Constraints (Thou shalt nots) come in the form of federal, state and local laws, other accreditation standards, and lack of resources in terms of funding, faculty and facilities. Resources are financial—tuition income, endowment, and other gifts; or human resources—faculty, staff, and administrators; as well as facilities—such as classrooms, laboratories, libraries etc.

Boundaries: Systems are "bounded." Just as our skin is the boundary of our human bodies, organizations have boundaries that determine who and what is outside the system and who or what is inside. For example, unless you are on the payroll or registered as a student or an alumnus, you are outside the USC system. The University has geographic boundaries and there are even bounds on the internet in terms of who may access the university and its courses, libraries etc. electronically.

Outputs: Things that flow out of USC are its outputs; these are things that leave the system, such as, students, research reports, former faculty, retirees, press releases etc. When the processor produces the above items, those items flow outside its boundary to become parts of its external environment.

Outcomes: Outputs have consequences! Outcomes are the longer term, downstream consequences that result from those things that have been processed by the University and left its boundaries. Graduates produce contributions to their professional areas and to society as a whole. Research results become the basis for meaningful inventions/innovations and improvements in the state of the art or best practices in the broader environment. The quality of a University's outputs can be evaluated based on consequences over a longer time horizon than simply publication dates, graduation day etc.

Measurement Channel: The outputs and outcomes of systems are measured to ascertain whether those systems are achieving their stated objectives. Examples in the Price School would be measures such as endowment funds raised, students graduated by degree objective, refereed articles published, and national rankings of the University and the Price School as a whole and for its individual degree programs.

System Manager: This term applies to whoever "steers" the system by evaluating measures and then exerting control by sending new inputs into the system. System managers may be University Presidents, Deans, Boards of Trustees, or Faculty Committees.

Goals: Universities have broad, continuing goals to produce quality graduates, research and community service. USC aspires to be a highly ranked research university with its component schools also being highly ranked in their respective fields. Attainment of some of its goals may be measurable, but seldom are goals achieved once and for all.

Objectives: Stated objectives are normally measurable and achievable in the relatively near future. For example, a specific objective for endowment fundraising can easily be measured, and one knows when the objective is attained. Fundraising campaigns usually persist until their objectives are attained. Similarly, quantitative and qualitative objectives can be set for student recruitment. Whether those objectives have been met can be ascertained as new academic years begin. Organizations and their component parts have numerous short term objectives that relate to their broader goals.

Feedback Systems are "steered" by their leaders. "System Managers" make use of Information feedback to assist them in their steering. Feedback is information including measures that flow back to system managers from the organization's outputs and outcomes. System managers can then compare the information and measures to the University's (School's) goals and objectives and decide what interventions they need to make via the "control channel".

Control Channel: Essentially, the manager's decisions based on feedback flow back into the processor as inputs such as changes in resource use, modified objectives, shifts in priorities etc. A useful analogy is to envision steering a ship; there are many similarities between steering a ship and leading an organization.

A Suggested Exercise

Readers are now challenged to select an organization or part of an organization that you are knowledgeable of and describe it as a system. You should attempt to do this by presenting a graphic depiction based on the systems diagram shown in Figure 2. In a page or two, provide examples of your chosen organization's inputs, processor, outputs etc. Or, if you prefer, you may simply place your examples on your graphic depiction.

Co-alignment Theory

James Thompson in his book, *Organizations in Action* (1967), identifies attaining co-alignment as the single most important function of organizational leaders. In the simplest of terms, an organization is co-aligned when it is in alignment with its external context. One can think of an organization as being co-aligned when it is compatible with or in harmony with forces in its external context.

The concept of co-alignment starts from the premise that organizations are "open systems" as opposed to being "closed systems" that are self-contained and impervious to their environments. Co-alignment models are "systems theory" based; they draw attention to interdependencies organizations have with individuals, groups, and organizations in their environments.

Based on extensive research, a co-alignment model was developed by John Kotter and Paul Lawrence in their book, *Mayors in Action*. The model was formulated at Simon's "individual layer" with its focus being Mayors of local governments. A modified co-alignment model appears below.

Modified Coalignment Model

General purpose model of Dodge Clinic behavior

The model depicts four contextual variables that I have modified for use at the organizational layer. (Permission for use of this model was provided by John Wiley & Sons, Inc. who hold the copyright for Mayors in Action authored by John Kotter and Paul Lawrence; this book was published in 1974).

The modified "contextual variables are:

- The Organization's Structure
- The Organization's Agenda

- The Organization's Network
- The Organization's Domain—its "turf"

The premise is that an organization needs to keep these variables "aligned" or "in harmony". These four contextual variables produce six relationships that need to be in alignment. (A straight line between two contextual variables indicates "alignment". A "ziggily" line indicates varying degrees of "non-alignment". In the Co-alignment model the more the "ziggles"—the greater the non-alignment.)

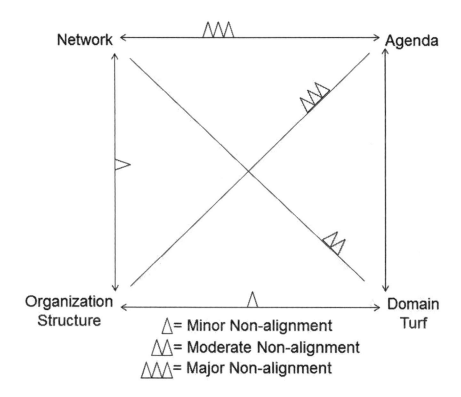

Assumptions regarding the six relationships are as follows:

An organization needs to have appropriate networks of individuals and organizations that will enable it to achieve its changing agenda.

The structure of the organization has to fit with its present or planned agenda (For example, a bureaucratic structure will not work well with an agenda calling for innovation). There are numerous ways to change an organization's behavior including structural consolidations, mergers and changing the organization's culture.

The domain or turf that the organization is seeking to impact, serve etc. should be reflected in its agenda. Changes in turf can include changing its clientele, geographic boundaries, and functional areas of work.

The organization's network should be congruent with its changing domain. Network nodes may need to be added or deleted to achieve the congruence.

The organization's structure should be in alignment with its network. Decentralized organizations will require network connections inclusive of individuals and units at lower levels in the organization.

The organization's structure should fit the domain it seeks to impact. Serving new clientele or providing new services requires structural change.

Over time the above six relationships invariably become non-aligned as changes occur within the organization and its context. Based upon Kotter and Lawrence's model (See the Circle in the Center of Figure 3), there are three processes that leaders can employ to modify these relationships to achieve alignment:

- Agenda Setting—revising the organization's agenda to accommodate changes in the contextual variables.

- Network Building—adding or dropping nodes on the network to reflect the organization's changing agenda. Nodes of networks may be individuals, groups or organizations. Networks are the source of resources, including political influence.

- Task Accomplishing—adjusting the organization's structure and behavior to facilitate accomplishing its agenda; for example, becoming more entrepreneurial, placing emphasis on being innovative, becoming less tied to bureaucratic procedures, creating new organizational units etc.

The system theory-based Co-alignment approach provides an additional "lens" for examining your organization's realities. Using this approach will shift your focus to your organization's changing context and to the implications of those contextual changes. In short, as noted above, the Co-alignment approach shifts the analytical focus from "Closed System" thinking to "Open System" thinking.

By thinking about your collaborative organization using the co-alignment approach, your focus is shifted to your organization's changing context and the implications of those contextual changes. This lens will cause you to think about such issues as:

- Is your definition of your organization's domain in need of revision given changes that are occurring in its context?

- Is the agenda that has been set to guide the organization's efforts appropriate to current and anticipated contextual changes?

- Is your organization's existing network what it should be? Is it sufficiently inclusive? Does it have the requisite strength/ connections to enable your organization to achieve its evolving agenda?

- Is your current organizational structure going to facilitate or impede carrying out the organizational agenda?

Suggested Exercise

Now that you have absorbed these illustrative discussions of the Co-alignment model, you are challenged to take the model and its underlying concepts and apply them to your own organization or another organization that you know well. Practice with application of the co-alignment model will help you with your understanding of both the model and your collaborative organization and should reassure you of your ability to make use of this powerful tool for system thinking.

I suggest that you develop a visual model. Your model should have a circle at its center that depicts the three organizational processes that can be used to move the organization toward co-alignment with its context. The model should also contain circles that depict the four contextual variables:

1. The Organization that is the focus of your analysis; how is it structured?
2. The Agenda of the organization
3. The Network of the organization
4. The Domain of the organization—what is its "turf"?

Your first challenge will be to describe the current degree of alignment that exists for the organization you are examining. Evaluate each of the six linkages as shown in Figure 4. Which of these are not in alignment at present? Assuming you find that some non-alignments exist, how serious are the non-alignments? (Show the degree of alignment with straight lines or lines with "ziggles" between the contextual variables as you see fit).

Your second challenge is to suggest strategies that the organization could adopt to eliminate non-alignments and perhaps achieve "co-alignment". (You may conclude that some degree of non-alignment of some of the linkages is inevitable.)

Once you have completed this exercise I think you will more readily grasp that the system theory-based Co-alignment Model provides you a valuable "lens" for examining your organization's status. The questions it should surface in your mind may have been only vaguely perceived in your thinking about your organization's problems and possible strategies to resolve them. This model should lead you to consider a broader range of possible strategies to employ in steering your organization along new paths.

In conclusion, this chapter has provided you with a language for systems thinking and two models you can make use of to improve your understanding of and ability to steer your organization. The next chapter will introduce you to another language, a language for role analysis. Acquiring an understanding of Role Theory and Role Analysis will be highly valuable to you in leading collaborative organizations.

Chapter 7

Language and Leadership

Vincent Ostrom

It is understandable that leaders in different nations speak in their native languages, but this is not the sense of the term, language, as used in this book. This chapter's focus on language considers it to be the terminology that leaders employ; that is, the concepts, metaphors, analogies, models etc. which leaders use, in the context of complex organizations and institutions, to think, act and communicate with their followers, peers, constituents etc.

S.I. Hayakawa, a Semanticist and a U.S. Senator for one term, authored a book addressing the role of *Language in Thought and Action*. Harcourt, Brace and Jovanovich published one of the multiple editions of his book in 1978; however, a less complete version of his work was published in 1939. This English Professor and former President of San Francisco State University was born in Canada of Japanese ancestry. There are multiple editions of his widely used book on this topic. Still, I was surprised that it was an assigned reading in my first week of a graduate course in Public Administration taught at the University of California at Los Angeles (UCLA).

I came to realize that Vincent Ostrom, the Professor who taught that course, was an original thinker who questioned much of conventional wisdom of that day regarding governance systems and public organizations. "Vince" did not equate organizations to bureaucratic structures. Instead he thought of organizations as simply constituting "predictable patterns of behavior". I was one of several graduate students who were fortunate enough to work with him on a Metropolitan Reform project he was engaged in along with other UCLA Professors, John Bollens, Winston Crouch, Ernest Englebert, and Charles Tiebout.

Professor Ostrom was skeptical of the value of the approaches to metropolitan reform that had currency in the late 1950's. Ostrom considered metropolitan regions as "Political Non-entities" (There were no governmental units that had boundaries coterminous with the metropolitan region) that manifested "predictable patterns of behavior" which he thought were most effectively studied by employing market based models that were grounded in the language of Economics and Business Administration. Much of his research at that time focused upon the "Lakewood Plan" by which smaller municipal governments contracted with the County of Los Angeles for delivery of some of their services. By employing a less conventional set of concepts and language, his research provided useful explanations for municipal behaviors in that era, and bases for suggesting ways to help shape those behaviors.

I share this brief example to explain the rationale for the reading assignment of Dr. Hayakawa's book noted above, but, more importantly, to reinforce one of the premises underlying this book; namely, that leaders need to become self-consciously aware of the extent to which the language, concepts etc. they employ in their thought and action processes have profound consequences for their perceptions of organizational realities and their effectiveness as leaders.

Language for Role Analysis

I will be illustrating this point in the remainder of this chapter by discussing the seminal book on Role Theory, *Explorations in Role Analysis*, written by N. Gross, W.S. Mason and A.W. McEachern and published by John Wiley and Sons in 1958. These scholars did their research for this book at Harvard University; they studied the (leader) behavior of School District superintendents in New England and in the process developed a highly useful language that has been employed over the years both in the conduct of research and by leaders in understanding role attributes and behaviors of themselves and of those who work around them. Professor McEachern was one of my esteemed faculty mentors while I was a Ph.D. student. Later he was a valued colleague on the faculty of the University of Southern California. This book was published by John Wiley & Sons in 1958; the publisher did not renew its copyright.

These Harvard researchers constructed a language for Role Analysis as noted below:

A Role Set is composed of a Focal Role such as a School Superintendent and Counter Roles such as School Board Members, Teachers, other Superintendents (peers), Classified Staff, State Department of Education officials, County level education officials, etc. A role set is depicted graphically below in Figure 5.

ROLE SET DIAGRAM

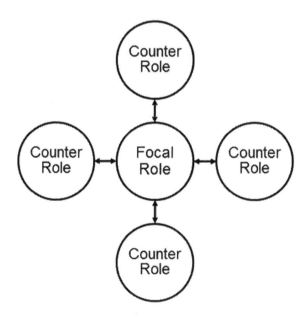

A Role is a Set of Expectations of an incumbent of a position (Such as a School Superintendent). Those expectations are expressed in the form of what the incumbent of (or applicant for) the role should or should not do or be. That is, what Behaviors should the incumbent be expected to perform/do or not perform/do; and what Attributes or Qualities should the incumbent have or not have. Examples of behaviors are: listening effectively, providing guidance to School Board members, and negotiating effectively with teachers and their unions. Examples of attributes are: being trustworthy, having negotiation skills, being empathetic etc.

These researchers' questionnaire, to be filled out by members of a Role Set, asks respondents to apply the following scale to a lengthy list of behaviors and attributes that the researchers had compiled while interviewing knowledgeable School Superintendents and School Board members. (The actual instrument is in the book cited above.)

The School Superintendent (or applicant):

1	2	3	4	5
Definitely Must	Probably Should	May or May Not	Preferably Should Not	Definitely Must Not

The respondents are then asked to assess the degree of importance they place on whether the incumbent of the role or the applicant for the role actually does have the particular attribute, quality or ability to behave/perform to meet each particular expectation. The scale for this assessment is shown below:

1	2	3	4	5
Of Extreme Importance	Of Major Importance	Of Moderate Importance	Of Minor Importance	Of No Importance

These responses are also analyzed and compared to the preferences noted above.

Responses are analyzed for the group of respondents as a whole and by the different clusters of Counter Roles that answered the questionnaire; that is the School Board Members, Teachers, Parents, Classified Employees, etc.

Finally, the respondents are asked to assess the degree to which the incumbent of the focal position's actual behaviors/attributes compare to the expected behaviors/attributes. Respondents indicate whether the incumbent has met or will meet a particular expectation: "Fully", For the Most Part, To Some Extent, or Not at All.

With the above description as backdrop we can now return to the "Language for Role Analysis.

- Role Prescriptions are made up of the entire set of expectations that are held for a role. These differ from the more common-place Job Descriptions which typically reflect only the views of a Supervisor or in this case a Board.

It should be noted that School Superintendents or candidates to become the incumbent of that position also hold expectations about the behaviors and attributes that they should have or be capable of performing. This is important to keep in mind as we lay out the rest of this useful language.

- Role Consensus exists when everyone's expectations of the incumbent of the Role are the same—a rare but desirable outcome.

- Role Conflict exists when expectations held for the Superintendent's Role are not the same—conflicting. The conflict reflects the differing views of the various groups in the Role Set, or it may reflect that the Superintendent/applicant views the Role differently from some of the groups in the role set. Role Conflict is frequently the case; the Harvard researchers found this to be the primary explanation for the high turnover rate among the School Superintendents they studied.

- Role Ambiguity exists when there is uncertainty regarding what is being expected of a Superintendent/Applicant. This may result from members of the Role Set being unclear about their expectations, or the School Superintendent may or may not be able to comprehend the set of expectations held for him or her. This problem frequently occurs because participants in the Role Set are poor Expectation Senders, or the School Superintendent is a poor Expectation Receiver. Over a period of time, a Superintendent can work to clear up these Role Ambiguities.

- Role Congruence exists when the expected behaviors/ attributes of the incumbent of a Focal Role match the actual behaviors/attributes of the incumbent. This is clearly what is desirable, but it may not be feasible depending upon the extent of conflicting expectations that are held.

Individual and group expectations are formed over time. Often, the way the previous incumbent of the Focal Role performed has shaped other members' of the Role Set's expectations as to how the role should be performed. This can be beneficial if the previous incumbent performed effectively. If not, expectations may have formed about what the next incumbent should not do or be. Such expectations will influence the selection and actual performance of new School Superintendents.

- Role Capabilities refers to an incumbent's capacity to live up to or exceed the expectations that are held for him or her.

- Role Sanctions refers to the rewards or punishments that may be meted out to a Superintendent based upon his role performance.

It needs to be noted that this Role Analysis Language can also be used to examine the Role of the School Board or for that matter, or any of the other Counter Roles such as Teachers etc. Expectations flow in many directions; for example, from the Board to the Superintendent, and from the Superintendent to the Board.

In this Chapter, I have attempted to illustrate that the language one employs leads to major differences in perceptions of what is going on in organizations. Using this language for role analysis will be of great utility in Inter-sectoral, collaborative organizations when they are being established and role ambiguity is not in short supply. Informal Role Analysis underlies much that goes on in non-hierarchical organizations. Having an explicit language for sorting things out both for the roles of individual employees and for the collaborative organization as a whole has much value.

Let me close by noting that there are many languages in play in organizations. For example, Public Choice Theory helps us to recognize where "moral hazards" exist, and alerts us to be wary of "shirkers" and "free riders". Decision Theories focus our attention on optimization or satisficing; rational choice, political and governmental process models each employ different assumptions about the likely behaviors of humans. Many of these analytical languages emanate from particular academic disciplines; they may be quite helpful to leaders, but let me reemphasize that they may create only partial pictures and may need to be supplemented with language from other disciplines. Leaders profit when they are at home with the use of multiple languages.

Chapter 8

Innovation:
An Exemplary "Collaborative Leader"
Dr. William B. McLean

This chapter first explores the nature of three interrelated processes: ideation, invention, and innovation. Everett Roger's insightful typology of the innovative behaviors of organizations is discussed as a backdrop for the case study contained in this chapter.

Next, analyze the leadership thoughts of one of the more noteworthy of our nation's inventors and innovators, Dr. William B. McLean. Bill McLean is best known as the inventor of the Sidewinder missile, but he made many other important contributions during his career and fostered the innovative capacity of two Naval Research and Development Laboratories while he served as their Technical Director. Dr. McLean is an exemplar of an "Ever Renewing" leader who was perpetually a few steps ahead of those working around him. His ability to inspire other professionals and instill in them a collaborative ethos was highly impressive.

The chapter concludes with the Story of the development of the Sidewinder Missile and its use in the Taiwanese Straits.

Permission to use excerpts from the Biographical Memoir of Dr. William B. McLean has been granted by the National Academy of Science, Courtesy of the National Academies Press.

Ideation, Invention and Innovation

It is useful to distinguish the above three terms. The definitions that I have most often encountered in the literature on the management of science and technology are:

- Ideation refers to the generation of ideas worthy of exploration for their potential utility/applicability. Inventions may flow from these ideas.

- Invention refers to the generation of new social or physical technologies that extend human and/or organizational capacities by providing new tools, instruments and techniques.

- Innovation refers to adopting an invention and bringing into actual use.

Leaders of organizations in general and inter-sectoral organizations in particular make choices in the way they design their organization's structures and processes. Their choices impact these three important capacities. Are their organizational designs and processes intended to reduce risk taking, enhance predictability, or to foster the organization's innovative capacity? Victor Thompson's classic book, *Bureaucracy and Innovation*, provides an insightful discussion of this leadership responsibility.

Everett Rogers in his book, *Communications and Innovation*, drives home the responsibility of leaders to make choices regarding their organizations' innovative behavior. Roger's insightful typology (classification scheme discussed below) demonstrates that organizations vary in the speed with which they decide to adopt new inventions after they become available.

Roger's typology raises the question, once a new technology is invented, how long does it take for it to diffuse (be innovated)? Organizations are placed into classes based on how quickly they choose to use new technologies as they come into being—are they "Innovators"?, "Early Adopters"?, "Early Majority"?, "Late Adopters"?, "Laggards"?, etc.? It is possible to classify organizations based upon their actual behaviors; however, it may be more important to find out what their leaders believe their classification should be. One can make the case that adopting a new technology too quickly may not be as good a choice as waiting until its usefulness can be judged based on what the experience of the "Innovators" or "Early Adopters" has been. A leader can readily defend a decision to have his/her organization fall in the "Early Majority" category for example.

I would argue leaders of inter-sectoral organizations, that are often temporary organizations, need to be alert to emergent opportunities to capitalize upon new technologies as they are invented and be "Innovators" or "Early Adopters" in their orientation. My view is that many of these organizations have similarities to projects/programs being conducted within Research and Development organizations; they should not be risk averse.

Next, this chapter will focus upon an Inventor, Dr. William B. McLean, as an exemplar, collaborative leader. McLean was the Technical Director of two large Naval R&D laboratories that consistently received top rankings among all government laboratories for their effectiveness. The organizational philosophies and leadership practices of McLean will be described and discussed in the sections which follow.

Dr. William B. McLean

This "case study" of an outstanding leader will draw upon a variety of sources:

Two Department of the Navy publications: *Sailors, Scientists and Rockets*, Volume, 1and *The Grand Experiment At Inyokern*, Volume 2. These volumes are histories of the Naval Weapons Center located at China Lake, California; they set the historical context for Dr. McLean's major technological achievements.

Dr. William H. Pickering's Biographical Memoir, written for the National Academy of Sciences to honor Dr. McLean shortly after his death, is drawn upon heavily. Dr. Pickering was a fellow graduate student at Cal Tech in the 1930's and interacted with Dr. McLean throughout his career. Dr. Pickering headed the Jet Propulsion Laboratory in Pasadena, California.

A collection of speeches and papers written while Dr. McLean was the Technical Director of the Naval Ordinance Test Station (NOTS)-now named the Naval Air Warfare Center. This collection was provided to me by Sterling Haaland who was the Deputy Commander for Research and Development of that Center in the early 1990's. An article in *Life Magazine* published on January 6, 1967 titled, "The Navy's Top Handyman" sheds light on McLean's leadership philosophies. Finally, my own personal knowledge of Dr. McLean during my eight years as an employee of the two Naval Laboratories he led as their Technical Director.

Dr. McLean's Personal Background

I cannot improve upon Dr. Pickering's description of Dr. McLean's personal background so I will simply quote it below.

"I first met Bill McLean when we were both graduate students at Caltech; and I grew to know and appreciate him some twenty years later when he was Technical Director of the Naval Ordnance Test Station at China Lake, California. For some twenty-five years thereafter I knew him as a scientist, engineer, inventor, and leader of men.

Bill was a highly principled and religious man, descended from a line of Presbyterian ministers. His maternal and paternal grandfathers, as well as his father and brother were ordained ministers. He often stated that he never felt a conflict between science and religion because he believed that all of knowledge was of a common origin, and that the highest function of the human intellect was the search for truth.

He was born in Portland, Oregon in 1914, but lived the first four years of his life in Dubuque, Iowa where his father was teaching. In 1919, the family moved to the Los Angeles area and lived in Eagle Rock where he completed his primary and secondary education. In 1931, he entered Caltech . . . . as an electrical engineer, but, after one term, Dr. Earnest Watson suggested he transfer to Physics. He received his B.S. in 1935 and the M.S. in 1937. His interests were experimental, particularly in the design of instruments. As a graduate student, he worked in nuclear physics with Dr. Charles Lauritsen and Dr. Willy Fowler on the construction of their half-million-volt Van der Graaff generator. He completed his Ph.D. in 1939 with a thesis on the short-range alpha particles produced by the bombardment of fluorine by 350 KEV protons . . . .

. . . . Shortly after receiving his Ph.D. degree, Bill married LaVerne Jones. LaV, as she was known, was the extrovert; Bill, the introvert. I had the pleasure to see them together at social gatherings; they were a remarkable couple who were treasured by lab employees and their families."

Dr. McLean's Professional Career

1939-   Received his Ph.D. in Physics from Caltech

1939-41   Held a Postdoctoral Fellowship in Nuclear Physics, University of Iowa where he worked on alpha particle counters, and instrumentation circuitry

1941-45   Bench Scientist-worked with proximity fuses, rockets, arming devices, fire control systems and acceleration integrators for the Bureau of Standards in Washington, D.C.

1945-68	Naval Ordnance Test Station, China Lake. Headed the Ordinance Division; then, the Aviation Ordinance Department; he became the Technical Director of the Laboratory in 1954
1968-74	Naval Undersea Center, San Diego, CA (now part of the Naval Command and Control Ocean Surveillance Center) Technical Director of the Center

Bill McLean's Achievements

Dr. McLean had innumerable achievements during his career. He acquired forty-nine patents, and was the recipient of many awards including the President's Award for Distinguished Federal Civilian Service. In 2008 a Navy Ship was name for him, the USSN William McLean. The ship is a Lewis and Clark dry cargo/ammunition ship. In 2010 a building was named in his honor. The 177,000 square foot McLean Laboratory is located at the Naval Air Warfare Center, China Lake, California. I recently had the opportunity to view the Center.

Among his more remarkable achievements were development of "CURV" and the Sidewinder missile. Dr. McLean's interest in underwater activities while still located in the desert at China Lake led to a program to build underwater, deep diving, cable controlled vehicles. This program produced CURV (a cable controlled underwater research vehicle). CURV was used in 1966 to recover the hydrogen bomb that was lost off the coast of Spain.

Dr. McLean's most well-known achievement is the Sidewinder air to air missile which uses infra-red radiation from the target airplane as the source of its guidance information. The development and first use of this missile is described in detail in the final section of this chapter. Let me simply note that with the strong support of President Eisenhower, the Navy awarded him $25,000 for his work on Sidewinder. At the award ceremony the Chief of Naval Operations, Admiral Arleigh A. Burke, stated that nothing since the Atomic Bomb had done so much for the Navy.

Leadership Attributes of Dr. McLean

The thesis underlying this section is that Dr. McLean provides an excellent role model for collaborative leaders as his own leadership philosophies and behaviors produced highly effective organizational cultures in each of the laboratories he led.

Dr. Pickering offers us a number of insights into Dr. McLean as a leader; he describes him as a scientist, engineer, inventor and leader of men. Pickering stated McLean was, "modest, soft-spoken, full of gentle humor, unremittingly honest, and stubbornly persistent when right". He labels McLean as an experimenter with a lifelong interest in "fixing things" and a particular interest in the design of instruments.

Pickering goes on to say that, "Bill was known for his low-key administration; he very seldom gave a direct order to his subordinates, and he did not try to dominate meetings. He had, however, the respect of his subordinates, and when he had something to say, they all listened. His technical understanding and creative imagination guaranteed his leadership".

Bill "aimed at as simple as possible solutions. He had the curiosity needed to ferret out the key factors in a problem, the wisdom to know what the important elements were in its solution, and the tenacity to stay with the problem until it was solved".

Dr. McLean's Leadership Beliefs

Dr. McLean favored the "type of management which maximizes enjoyment, participation and the contributions of individual creativity, rather than the type of management whose goals and objectives are set at the top . . . . without consideration of possible creative inputs". A theme he often expressed in meetings was, "the less management the better". My colleague and good friend, Frank Sherwood once spent some time as a consultant observing "NOTS" and concluded it was in practice very much a "bottom up organization". McLean once told Sherwood that he (McLean) had no need to intercede in the management of the Laboratory, it runs itself! In fact, the organizational culture which he helped to create provided mission clarity and goal commitments much like Follett's discussion of "Invisible Leaders"

McLean also clearly understood that among his important duties was serving as a buffer between the Lab's technical employees and their work, and bureaucratic rules and regulations. McLean protected both the time of his technical employees and their sense of freedom to think creatively about their projects.

An interesting organizational philosophy of Dr. McLean relates to organizational aging; he believed that organizations lose their creative capacities over time. His view was that after an organization has been around for twenty years or more, it should be closed down or moved a couple of hundred miles away so that it could be infused with new people and fresh ideas. Bill did not use the terminology, but it is clear from his statements that he recognized the need for renewal at both the organizational and individual levels. In fact, his own move from China Lake to San Diego which involved major shifts of personnel between Navy laboratories was in essence, "walking his talk".

Bill would have been in agreement with Caltech Economist, Burton Klein, who enunciated a management principle that, "you use up strangeness to generate new ideas". The periodic rotation of his top department heads to different departments and the annual infusion of highly motivated "Junior Professional" employees reflected this principle. In fact, McLean favored a high internal turnover rate with scientists and engineers moving around the laboratory with some frequency. The fact that projects being worked on within the laboratory were in regular flux was also helpful in this regard.

In a lecture for the Engineering School of the University of California at Berkeley McLean asserted that, "designing a successful missile is similar to completing a mural in that the finished creation reflects primarily the skill, ability, and experience of the master artist, but . . . . also uses the individual skills of his assistants to a maximum.

The story of Sidewinder attests to the maverick tendencies of Dr. McLean. In one of his speeches he commented that "China Lake can and should take advantage of the freedom we have because of the lack of continuity and organizational confusion in Washington, if we have the courage and vision necessary to exercise it". McLean strongly supported the nurturing of creative scientists and argued against stressing productivity at the expense of risk taking. Employees in our technical organizations might be said to work for me—"as much as anyone ever works for anyone in a technical organization. Let's say, that I can protect them from being directed".

Dr. McLean had a strong personal network that included many of the Navy's top officers. It is my understanding that when a newly arrived Captain became the Commanding Officer of "NOTS" and began to intrude himself into management of the technical work of the Laboratory, Dr. McLean contacted members of his network and the Commanding Officer was reassigned within days.

In another speech McLean pleads, "We need to find some way to rescue the design of our military equipment from the morass of integration, coordination, centralization and detailed specifications in which it is now sinking".

In the *Life Magazine* article noted above McLean is quoted as saying, "that when we stop being different and nonconformist, our output will stop too." McLean goes on to note in this article that "The most useful money that we have, is the 5% of our budget that is allotted for otherwise unsupported projects. Almost all of our major developments get started that way. I find that the normal budgetary cycle is a very poor process for trying out new ideas."

When asked how do you get an idea? McLean answered, "I haven't the foggiest notion. You start working on something interesting, and as you go along, you keep getting ideas that change it."

Another interesting McLean observation shared with *Life's* correspondent, John Riley, is that, "I don't think I've ever seen a useful piece of equipment produced by the 'normal procedure'— the idea that you first write a specification and then expect the laboratory to fulfill it. As Admiral Mahan said, you don't start with a military requirement. You start with the new equipment and develop the tactics to match its characteristics."

McLean was a systems thinker who attributed much of the success of the China Lake lab to the fact that it had many of the elements of the design process in one location; that is, basic and exploratory research, each of the stages of development, engineering capabilities including well equipped machine shops, and test and evaluation resources. McLean was a strong advocate of the government doing its own R&D in Civil Service Laboratories, with industry's role primarily in the production area; he felt that these labs provided needed benchmarks for cost and quality, and the competencies required to ensure that taxpayers were getting their money's worth from the private sector. Unfortunately this philosophy has not prevailed over the years as a result of ongoing, persistent lobbying of our elected officials.

The results of Dr. McLean's leadership philosophies are well illustrated in the following story of the Sidewinder missile and Taiwan.

The Sidewinder Missile and the Taiwanese Straits

The Sidewinder missile was first used in combat over the Taiwanese Straits in September of 1958. Up until that time military aircraft relied primarily upon rockets which, when fired, lacked guidance systems and were not particularly accurate or reliable weapons. The Sidewinder was a dramatic advancement in air-launched weaponry and, subsequent to the Taiwan incident, was adopted by the U.S. Air Force and over a dozen of our allied nations. We will begin this story by describing the Sidewinder missile. Then, we will discuss the ideation, invention and innovation processes that preceded the deployment and use of this remarkable weapon.

The Sidewinder is named after a deadly desert rattlesnake. The missile is five inches in diameter and nine feet long! It travels at supersonic speed, and can change course in flight. The guidance system homes upon the heat from the tail pipe of its target aircraft. It is a highly reliable, effective weapon. Because of its low cost of production and ease in use, there are thousands of these missiles available to our forces and to our allies.

There have been numerous modifications over the years to upgrade the Sidewinder. Many other missiles have been developed that build upon the technologies underlying Sidewinder and extend them to other operational requirements of the military such as ground to air weapons. However, along the path to its initial development and use, many obstacles were encountered by its "Master Craftsman". Dr. McLean and his supporters had to battle hard to bring the Sidewinder to fruition. Dr. Pickering in his memorial to Dr. McLean said, "I feel it is not too much of an exaggeration to assert that Bill built Sidewinder in spite of the Navy"!

This story begins with Dr. McLean's habit of walking in the desert at night. As he frequently encountered Sidewinder snakes with their distinctive movements from side to side, his curiosity was aroused by the fact that these snakes hunt their prey in relative darkness. How is it, he asked, that they can successfully track their prey?

Laboratory lore is that McLean consulted with Biologists and learned that the Sidewinder snake's head contains infra-red sensing organs which enable it to track heat trails left by its animal prey. This knowledge stimulated a question on McLean's part, could he develop a heat seeking mechanism that could improve upon current rocket technologies? Could he incorporate a heat seeking capacity into a guidance system that could be coupled with other elements that would be required to produce a missile; e.g., an air frame, propulsion system, warhead, control system, etc.? McLean had the vision to see the enormous potential of a missile with this capability. The process of invention was quickly underway.

McLean was taking on major technological challenges, and he quickly encountered multiple bureaucratic and political obstacles. No general or specific operational requirements for such a missile had been issued by any of the Navy Department's multiple Bureaus. There were no appropriated funds to tap. In the early stages of the Sidewinder's development McLean could make use of some Exploratory Research funding. Since the NOTS lab was under a modified industrial funding system, there was also some flexibility to charge costs to General and Area Overhead funds. I suspect there were also charges that managed to get shifted to the Job Orders of other projects underway in the lab, and many unpaid, volunteer hours of effort were committed to the Sidewinder. Nonetheless, this development effort was taking place without its own funding or the legitimacy implied by having its own headquarters authorized funding.

Word of the Sidewinder effort soon reached Washington D.C. The various Navy Bureaus were contenders for the Naval Department's budget. There was great reluctance on the part of most of the Bureaus to add another unauthorized contender to their budgetary battles. McLean was told to cease his work on the Sidewinder. Congress got into the act and sent staff to investigate whether work on Sidewinder had in fact stopped. Laboratory lore has it that McLean was told that if he did not stop the lab's work on the Sidewinder, he would be going to jail! But, work continued!

McLean's major problem was that his missile needed to be flight tested which required use of instrumented flight ranges and aerial photography; this required a sizable expenditure of funds which he did not have. The Air Force stepped up to this challenge and quietly allowed the flight testing to be done on its ranges. The missile's reliability was reputedly 95 percent and may have been higher!

The first use of the Sidewinder (Its innovation) occurred in 1958 in the Taiwanese Straits. At that time the very existence of the Sidewinder was classified so little information about the missile and this incident became public. The Director of Naval History declassified some information about Sidewinder in March of 1980. An unidentified

Nationalist Chinese Fighter Pilot provided a first-hand account of the air battle that occurred on September 24, 1958. His account is available in a book titled, *Fighter Pilot*, by Major Stanley M. Ulanoff that was published by Doubleday and Company in 1962. The story recounted below is based upon Laboratory lore; an article in the *Rocketeer*-the newspaper published by the China Lake Laboratory; an Associated Press story published on October 17, 1958 and some status reports that were declassified by the Naval Historian.

In the summer of 1958 intelligence reports indicated that the Mainland Chinese government was massing its fleet of naval vessels in preparation for an invasion of Formosa (Taiwan). Air reconnaissance flights were being conducted in advance of the planned invasion. The Nationalist Chinese Air Force had aging F86 planes; the Mainland Chinese had modern MIG17s. Air superiority clearly belonged to the Mainland Chinese.

The story goes that President Eisenhower called in his top military advisors and told them that he wanted the planned invasion stopped, and he did not want to involve the United States directly. Reputedly, one of the Military Chiefs asked, "Mr. President, How are we going to do that?" President Eisenhower reportedly bristled and said, "I am the President; you are the military leaders. I want you back here tomorrow with a plan of action".

The next day when the Chiefs returned, the Chief of Naval Operations told the President that there was a scientist named McLean that had under development an unauthorized missile that is reported to be a major advance in the technology for aerial warfare. Perhaps we could make it available to the Nationalist Chinese? The President reacted positively indicating this idea had his full support.

The Laboratory at China Lake jumped into action. A team of engineers flew to Taiwan to examine the F86s and measure and assess them in order to design and build racks for carrying and launching Sidewinder missiles. The racks were built by the Engineering Department using the Lab's machine shops. Then, the racks were flown to Taiwan, and China Lake engineers installed them and made other necessary equipment modifications. A first increment of 20 planes was completed by September 12, 1958. Pilot training commenced; fortunately, the Sidewinder was very easy to employ and only minimal training was necessary. Successful test firings were soon accomplished. Just 60 days after the President blessed this undertaking, the Nationalist Chinese Air Force was ready.

On September 24 a group of eight F86s encountered 20 MIG jets and combat began. Eight more F86s joined the fray and there were approximately 100 MIGs in the air. The Nationalist air force reported shooting down 10 MIGs and possibly, one more. All of the F86s returned to their bases. Air superiority was suddenly resting with the Nationalists. Within days the Mainland China Navy dispersed its massed fleet, and the threat of invasion ended. One can imagine the tremendous uncertainty this air battle created for the Mainland Chinese. Why were their superior aircraft defeated? Some-time later Secretary of State, John Foster Dulles, disclosed that the Nationalists had used Sidewinder missiles; the Communist Chinese protested with no result; they were more than a little anxious to learn more about the Sidewinder.

As noted earlier, President Eisenhower gave Dr. McLean the President's Award for Distinguished Federal Civilian Service, and the Department of the Navy gave him a $25,000 cash award. McLean used the award for equipment he could use in his home garage to continue his experiments and inventive practices! The Sidewinder is a dramatic story; I use it with intent to convey how a dedicated leader with a clear sense of purpose can overcome obstacles placed in his path. Inspiration and perspiration are likely to be attributes of successful collaborative leaders!

In the final chapter which follows a summary and some concluding observations are offered.

Chapter 9

Summary and Conclusion

When two or more organizations from different sectors (Private, Public and Not-for-Profit agree to collaboratively undertake programs or projects that can't be carried out by a single sector, a "collaborative organization" will be formed. These collaborative organizations pose many challenges for their leaders. The primary purpose of this book has been help those leaders better understand these organizations and their challenges so that they will be effective leaders, learners and disseminators of insights to future collaborative leaders.

The premises underlying this book were identified in Chapter 1. One premise is that Research and Development organizations with their multiple programs and projects and non-hierarchical, horizontal organizational structures provide useful comparison models for collaborative organizations. Leaders of R&D laboratories and the programs and projects within them face many of the same challenges as leaders of collaborative organizations.

Next, a number of the important characteristics of collaborative organizations were identified along with some of the leadership challenges those characteristics entail. Then, literature on leadership, and organization and management theory was perused in an effort to provide leaders assistance in dealing with their challenges. Landmark writings on leadership were explored for useful insights.

Readers were then exposed to the nature of organization and management theory and its building blocks: concepts, maps, models, theories, lens and frames. The importance of the language leaders employ in their thinking and action processes was noted. Leaders were encouraged to be more self-aware of their receptive and preceptive thought processes. Conceptual tools to facilitate leaders' thought processes were identified and discussed including a language for role analysis, system diagrams, and co-alignment models.

Chapter 8 contained a case study of an exemplary collaborative leader, Dr. William B. McLean, the Technical Director of two Navy Laboratories and a noted inventor. The story of one of his inventions, the Sidewinder missile, and its impact on the nation of Taiwan is recounted.

I have advanced the thesis in this book that leading collaborative organizations is a highly challenging undertaking that requires the ability to think and act in the midst of situations that are highly turbulent and when available information is only partial at best. Since by definition, collaborative leaders cannot rely upon hierarchical authority; these highly skilled leaders will be challenged to act based upon their experienced-based personal judgments and their capacity to inspire others to behave collaboratively. In my mind there is an emergent professional calling for those who would take on collaborative leadership roles. This role will proved demanding, but it also promises to be highly rewarding. As a society experiencing increasing complexity, we will need individuals who can rise to this challenge and provide the leadership that our collaborative organizations will require.

In my view, collaborative organizations are going to become increasingly important to societies around the world, and perhaps, particularly in our own country given the growing interdependence of the three sectors. Leaders of collaborative organizations will fill a critical role for society; it is important that they work hard to become effective collaborative leaders. These leaders will need to capitalize upon their rich experiences in leading collaborative organizations; they will need to learn from their leadership experiences, act based on that learning and act again while sharing what they are learning with future collaborative leaders. In addition, these leaders will need to be "ever renewing" as individuals and facilitators of their organizations becoming "ever renewing" as well!

Appendix

Written by John Shirey, City Manager of Sacramento

Use of Public-Private Partnerships (P3s)

Introduction

It is not always easy to tell which new public management ideas will gain long-term utility or merely fade from the scene after short-term popularity. Think of the many attempts to reinvent public sector budgeting: program budgeting; planning, programming, budgeting system (PPBS); and zero-based budgeting. In retrospect, all seem to have been just management fads. (In fairness, some elements of each have lived on in newer methods of budgeting.)

However, some management ideas seem to recycle every so many years. One of those is public-private partnerships, or P3s, as they have come to be called.

Such arrangements seem to be all the rage these days, but despite what some people would have us believe, public-private partnerships as a way for government entities and private businesses to work together to achieve a common good are not new. While perhaps not previously referred to as P3s, they have been in use for literally centuries in the United States.

An early example is the Lancaster Turnpike, a toll road built by the private sector with government oversight and publicly-owned rights of way. It opened in Pennsylvania in 1793. Other similar examples include the Erie Canal, which opened in 1825, and, of course, the

First Transcontinental Railroad completed in 1869 at Promontory Summit, Utah.

In their latest comeback, P3s seem to have gained new life about 2008 when the Great Recession took hold and governments found themselves with shrinking resources coupled with ongoing or expanding needs in all areas. At about the same time, enterprising consultants and advisors found this "new" product to sell to public administrators desperate to find alternative ways to conduct economic development, address transportation problems, build water and sewer infrastructure, deliver social services, and meet countless other public needs.

Advantages

While public-private partnerships have their share of critics who claim they amount to nothing more than needless public subsidies for private businesses, when used prudently P3s offer distinct advantages. In an era of declining public resources, P3s may provide the ability to increase revenues without raising taxes. There may be insufficient private dollars to complete the project or the return on investment may be so marginal that a private entity is not willing to shoulder 100% of the risk.

P3s bring about maximization of public funds by leveraging additional private funds. Such collaboration can lead to public officials and business persons working together for a common purpose rather than working at cross-purposes, as is sometimes the case.

In some instances, the partnership can lead to a better measure of control over a government project or program than if the private sector were left to proceed on its own.

In the end, the purpose of public-private partnerships should be to improve public services, programs, or projects, and provide additional assets to a community. The goal is a better outcome, one that results in a superior product over what could be accomplished if either the public or private sector acted alone.

Types of P3s

The only limit on the types of public-private partnerships that may be utilized to address countless public sector needs is one's imagination. For purposes of discussion here, though, we will put some framework around the types of partnership structures.

Probably the simplest of all arrangements is the straight-forward **Private Contract for Services**. In a contract relationship, the government entity buys a service or pays a private company to operate and/or maintain a facility the government believes it cannot operate as economically or efficiently. Many cities and counties, for example, contract with private waste haulers to collect residential/commercial refuse. A variation on this type is "performance contracting" in which the private contractor gets paid only if it meets certain performance contracting criteria such as an ambulance company contracted to respond to emergency medical calls within a specified time.

Another familiar type of partnership is the **Design-Build** process. In this case, the public entity wants a facility built but needs to speed up the process. It does that by combining two traditional steps—the design phase and the construction phase—into one by hiring a contractor to build as it designs. This usually saves money as well as time. One caveat: this consolidation does not always work well for complex projects requiring a special skill set to complete the design work.

In both private contracts and design-build projects, there may be circumstances requiring rapid completion of a project to avoid disruptions. In such cases, it may be warranted to offer contractors financial incentives to ensure projects stay on schedule. When the Santa Monica Freeway in Los Angeles had to be repaired following a serious earthquake and when a stretch of Interstate 5 in downtown

Sacramento had to be rebuilt to avoid possible flooding, highway engineers needed to get the work done while minimizing closures of heavily-traveled interstates. In these projects the contractors were offered financial bonuses for each day the projects were completed ahead of schedule. In both cases the contractors found ways to cut time from the projects and earned sizeable financial payments as a result!

There are many variations on the Design-Build process, such as **Design-Build-Operate-Maintain.** As the name suggests, the private entity has the responsibility to operate and maintain the facility after it designs and builds it. An example might be a new water treatment plant. One advantage of this arrangement is that since the private company has to operate and maintain what it builds, it has an incentive not to cut corners during the design and construction phases. The public entity usually owns the facility and may still bear responsibility for financing it.

An obvious variation on this type of P3 is **Design-Build-Finance-Operate** in which the private entity also has to provide the financing for the project. An example of a project built this way is the Dulles Greenway outside of Washington, D.C., a 14-mile toll expressway in Northern Virginia leading to Dulles International Airport.

Yet another option is **Build-Own-Operate** in which the government entity grants the right to a private company to own the improvement after building it and continuing to operate it. This form is not common because of the obvious disadvantage of the government losing control of the facility or operation.

A much more common type of P3 is the **Long-Term Lease Agreement.** In this type, a publicly-owned asset is leased to a private entity for a long period of time (perhaps as long as 99 years) and the private party is responsible for operating and maintaining the asset. The private entity may be required to pay a sum of money upfront for the right to lease the asset long-term. The key in these transactions is that the government owner receives fair value for its asset while leaving enough of a financial incentive for the private entity to properly operate and maintain the facility at a reasonable profit. Such valuations are difficult to determine for leases extending several decades.

Creative Uses of P3s

In recent years, P3s have been used in more creative ways than traditional approaches to using them for building infrastructure and facilities. One example is their use for developing affordable housing, particularly in high-cost areas such as most of California. When costs of land, building supplies, labor, and a reasonable profit are factored in to the proformas in a high cost area, the result can be that the housing is not affordable to low—and moderate-income families living in the area. Thus, while the need is high, the project won't be built. One solution is to use a P3.

While there are countless specific examples of this approach, a general outline of such a transaction with a non-profit or for-profit developer could involve the public entity buying the land and writing down its cost to the developer. Both parties may work together to secure financing for the housing which often involves several sources of funds, each with its own limitations. The public entity may help expedite the processing of entitlements and building permits, thus saving time and money. The developer then designs, builds, and operates the project. Property taxes on the completed project may be waived or deferred as another part of the financing to make it affordable to the new renters or owners.

Another creative approach to using P3s is to encourage economic development in urban areas. For example, one of the disincentives for the private sector to develop retail uses in older downtown areas is the cost of providing parking. In suburban or "greenfield" areas, land is most often cheaper by comparison and parking can be provided on surface-level parking lots, usually for free to shoppers. To "level the playing field" between the two types of geographic areas and to encourage more in-fill development where it makes the most sense, the public entity may enter into an agreement with the private developer to finance and/or build structured public parking that will also serve the retail development. The parking garage may also serve multiple uses in the area.

Social purposes could also be served in the above transaction. For example, the public partner could require the private partner to provide an apprenticeship training program during the construction phase so that local unemployed persons could learn construction skills and become employable in the future.

Cautions

It may seem to a public administrator that entering into a public-private partnership to procure a service or build a facility is considerably easier than accomplishing the same end with government employees. That may well be, particularly if in-house personnel or personnel with the right skills are not available. However, deciding to use a P3 does not mean no work is involved. Quite the contrary.

The key to any good public-private partnership is a well-crafted written contract or agreement that spells out the responsibilities of the parties, the deliverables, and the remedies if all does not go smoothly. Having a good contract actually starts with developing the document that will be used to solicit proposals or bids from private entities. Such solicitations may take the form of Requests for Qualifications (RFQs), Requests for Proposals (RFPs), or formal bid solicitations.

Briefly, RFQs simply solicit the qualifications and experience of firms for the job to be done. RFPs not only ask for qualifications but also formal proposals for how the respondents would provide the service or project, with or without estimates for their costs of providing the service or building the project. Formal Bid solicitations ask companies to offer a firm price for the service or project wanted according to detailed specifications, and the successful bidder is usually based on the lowest cost. The latter are normally not used to choose partners for P3s because in P3s other factors besides cost need to be considered by the government partner.

Whether using RFQs or RFPs, it is essential that the solicitation documents be as specific as possible so that the government can make fair comparisons between the respondents. Very often there will be an initial screening of the responses to eliminate those who are clearly unsuited for the project followed by oral interviews before a panel of evaluators for those who submit strong responses.

After the selection of the successful proposer, the parties enter into negotiations to formulate the contractual agreement. Depending on the skill levels of in-house staff, it may be advisable to hire special counsel and/or consultants to assist in the negotiations and development of the contract. It may also be advisable to hire experts to write the original RFP, to develop various background materials, and to assist in the evaluation of responses. It may even be necessary to hire outside experts to oversee the performance of the private partner. P3s, if done haphazardly, can get governments in trouble; it is important to have the expertise in place on the side of the government to prevent that from happening.

While public-private partnerships offer many advantages to governments, things can go wrong. A notorious example is the recent transaction by the City of Chicago to turn over control of its parking garages and on-street parking spaces to a private company in exchange for a large upfront sum of money. The private company quickly raised parking rates so high that Chicago citizens protested. Moreover, many experts believe that Chicago did not receive adequate compensation for the value of its parking assets. To make matters worse, Chicago used the money to reduce budget deficits though it is never a good practice to use one-time money to address ongoing expenses.

Chicago's example may be extreme, but problems can occur with any P3. P3s can be controversial, too, since they are usually done without competitive bidding because partnerships are negotiated.

In addition, in most P3s, the government (i.e. the public) is giving up some measure of control over a service, program, or facility.

There are many decisions to be made when entering into a P3. Returning to the simple example above about the local government that decides to contract for refuse collection, there are several options to consider. Will the private party collect commercial as well as residential waste? What recyclables will be collected, and in what way? Will the service be provided jurisdiction-wide or limited to a specific geographical area? Will collections be made on holidays? What should be the standards for the equipment used and how well it is maintained? Will the contractor do the billing or will the government retain that responsibility? Which party will take customer complaints? And a myriad of other issues!

Conclusion

It is incumbent upon any public administrator who decides to use a P3 to always ask the hard questions:

- Is the transaction of mutual benefit to both parties?
- Are taxpayers receiving a fair return on their money?

As emphasized above, to avoid problems and controversies, public administrators need to ensure they have surrounded themselves with the expertise to objectively evaluate any P3 arrangement.

When done properly, though, P3s can be an answer to making public resources go further and to achieve greater public good.

Bibliography

Chester Barnard, *The Functions of the Executive (Cambridge, Mass: Harvard University Press, 1938.)*

Warren Bennis, *The Essential Bennis* (San Francisco: Jossey-Bass, 2009.)

Lee G. Bolman and Terrence E. Deal, *Reframing Organizations: Artistry, Choice and Leadership* (San Francisco: Jossey—Bass, 1984 and 2008.)

John Gardner, *On Leadership (New York: Simon and Schuster, 1993.)*

Neal Gross, Ward S. Mason, and Alexander W. McEachern, *Explorations in Role Analysis* (New York: John Wiley and Sons, 1966.)

Luther Gulick and Lyndall Urwick, editors, *Papers on the Science of Administration* (New York: Institute for Public Administration, 1937.)

Charles A. Kepner and Benjamin B. Tregoe, The Rational Manager *(New York: McGraw-Hill, 1965.)*

John P. Kotter and Paul R. Lawrence, *Mayors in Action* (New York: John Wiley and Sons, 1974).

Henry Metcalf and Lyndall Urwick, editors, *Dynamic Administration: the collected papers of* Mary Parker Follett. (New York: Harper and Row, 1942.)

Roland McKean, *Efficiency in Government through Systems Analysis* (New York: John Wiley and Sons, 1958.)

Charles Hitch and Roland McKean, *The Economics of Defense in the Nuclear Age* (Cambridge, Mass: Harvard University Press, 1960.)

Richard Neustadt, *Presidential Power* (New York: John Wiley and Sons, 1960.)

John M. Pfiffner and Frank P. Sherwood, Administrative Organization (Englewood Cliffs, NJ: Prentice Hall, 1961.)

Everett M. Rogers, *The Diffusion of Innovations* (New York: The Free Press, 1962.)

Steven Sample, *The Contrarian's Guide to Leadership* (San Francisco: Jossey-Bass, 2002.)

Donald Schon, *Beyond the Stable State* (New York: W. W. Norton & Company, 1973.)

Donald Schon, *The Reflective Practitioner* (New York: Basic Books, 1984.)

Frederick W. Taylor, *The Principles of Scientific Management (New York: Harper and Brothers, 1911.)*

James Thompson, Organizations in Action *(New Brunswick, NJ: Transaction Publishers, 1967 and 2003.)*

Victor Thompson, Bureaucracy and Innovation *(Tuscaloosa, AL: University of Alabama Press, 1969.)*

Max Weber, author; Guenther Roth, Claus Wittich, editors, Economy and Society (Berkeley, CA: University of California Press, 1922 and 1978.)

Norbert Wiener, Cybernetics (Cambridge, Mass: MIT Press, 1948.)

21748563R00060

Made in the USA
San Bernardino, CA
04 January 2019